JEANNE ANCELET-HUSTACHE

Translated by Cecily Hastings

Goethe

Evergreen Profile Book 5

GROVE PRESS, INC.
NEW YORK

JOHN CALDER
LONDON

FIRST PUBLISHED IN THIS EDITION 1960. ALL RIGHTS RESERVED.

Library of Congress Catalog Card Number: 59-7437

Evergreen Profile Books are published

in the United States by Barney Rosset at Grove Press Inc.

64 University Place   New York 3, N.Y.

in Great Britain by John Calder (Publishers) Ltd.

17 Sackville Street   London, W. 1

Distributed in Canada by McClelland & Stewart Ltd., 25 Hollinger Rd., Toronto 16

First published in France by Editions du Seuil, Paris

MANUFACTURED BY MOUTON & Co., IN THE NETHERLANDS

Goethe
by Jeanne Ancelet-Hustache

Contents

I. One hundred and forty-three octavo volumes

Goethe never stopped writing, from his childhood to the eve of his death at the age of eighty-two. The great Weimar edition of his works consists of one hundred and forty-three octavo volumes: sixty-three of what may properly be called his works, sixteen of his private diaries, fourteen of scientific writings, and fifty of letters. Nor does this include the five large volumes of 'conversations'—the great man's spoken words, so far as his faithful hearers have transmitted them to posterity; nor certain texts, believed to have been lost, and in some cases essential to the writing of an intimate biography, which have been recovered, thanks to a happy chance, after years of neglect in indifferent hands.

There was never a man in whose life the work to be done played a more dominant part; nor one whose literary work leaves less room for any dissociation of the writer from the man. One of the greatest lyric poets of modern times, he provides a striking illustration of the law of the species. From his first adventure to his last despairing and renunciatory love affair, it was what moved him which gave the matter for his song. 'All my poems are occasional poems, stimulated by the reality which gave rise to them.' He conferred the quality of duration upon the fleeting

5

moment, an external 'occasion' providing the initial shock needed to set his affective powers in motion.

In a wider sense, the plays, novels and epics, and even the writings on artistic and literary criticism and in scientific subjects, are equally 'occasional' works. Goethe's characters have the vitality of Shakespeare's, and would live with a life of their own, however ignorant the reader might be of their intimate ties with their creator. But we do, as it happens, know practically all the 'occasions' which brought them into existence, so that an extra, historical value is added to the value of the work in its own right.

Such was the beginning [i.e., in his eighteenth year] *of that course from which I have been unable throughout my whole life to deviate: I mean the conversion of whatever delighted, distressed or otherwise preoccupied me into an image, a poem, thus finishing with it; so as both to rectify my notions of exterior things, and to tranquillize myself interiorly. There can hardly be anyone with more need than I of the gift of doing this, possessing as I do a nature which constantly drives me from one extreme to the other. Everything of mine which has appeared so far consists only of fragments of a great confession, which this little book is a bold attempt to complete.* (Dichtung und Wahrheit, *Book vii;* his memoirs, and in no sense a 'little' book!)

So, whether expressed in the inspiration of the moment or in the retrospective analysis of old age, it is Goethe himself who is everywhere present. And this does not apply only to his lyrics. Nor does it apply only to such characters as are obvious projections of himself at some particular moment of his life—Prometheus, Werther, Tasso, Wilhelm Meister, and, at every stage of his life, Faust—but also to those which reflect a more secret aspect of himself: the 'second soul' of which Faust speaks, contrasting it with the soul athirst for the absolute; that which harbors within itself a tangled mixture of the positivism of Antonio and William of Orange, the infidelities of Weislingen and Clavigo, Mephistopheles' sarcastic laughter and Orestes' frenzies under the persecution of the Furies.

His work expresses everything a man is given along with himself: his destiny, his genius, his *daemon*: 'You cannot be otherwise than thus, you cannot escape yourself. The daemon persists through everything; call him your own nature, or the old Adam, or what you will—each time he is expelled he returns, more uncontrollable than ever.'

But this is, at the same time, a perpetual process of becoming, because organic metamorphosis, 'duration in change' is the law of life itself, as he suggests in his poem of that name, *Dauer im Wechsel*: autumn storms scatter the leaves to which the flowers gave place; all things change, and you cannot bathe twice in the same stream.

Goethe with all his contradictions. For Valéry, discovering them amounted 'almost to a game,' so that he came to wonder whether Goethe 'had not adopted a system of cultivating direct opposites.' As though it were a question of deliberate decisions of the will! What human being, with or without genius, can always recognize himself as the same creature? How much more a poet, who is more subject than others to momentary impressions, and projects hundreds of images outside himself. An historian may pore over the dead letter of the texts, pointing a critical finger at each apparent contradiction. But life sweeps the living man 'from one extreme to the other.' However, whereas most men are quite unconcerned at such alternations, Goethe fought an unceasing battle to find the point of equilibrium between his own antagonisms.

Hence his life and his work—which are one thing—give an effect of polyphony, and different people, each remembering those themes by which he was particularly struck, pass judgments upon him which range from the quasi-idolatrous to the unbelievably severe. Pagan, mystical, sensual, sublime, 'Olympian'—they are all appropriate adjectives, as are many more besides. What is marvelous and unique in Goethe is that, for those who listen more attentively, so many of the dissonances find a resolution in harmony.

There is no poet whose life is better known. Yet who can flatter himself that he knows Goethe, even after a life-time's acquaintance with him?

There are the plain material reasons, for a start. The mere titles of the works written about him fill two large octavo volumes; twenty-two thousand of them by 1912! For France alone, the figure is four hundred and twenty-nine in the period from 1912 to 1948. His works set more problems than can be solved in a single lifetime. The specialists sometimes dream of monographs produced by team-work. But since each would only be able to judge with his own personal temperament, however firmly they might aim at objectivity, the result could only be a composite image with a few extra, gratuitous contradictions thrown in.

Then there are the more intimate reasons. In Goethe, as in every soul, there is the ultimate, unapproachable mystery, which he himself constantly and jealously preserved. He repeatedly insists on his preference for remaining incognito; to Schiller, he professes his desire to interpose another image of himself between his own personality and the eyes of the reader. He is very willing to talk, but he stops at the point where he has decided to stop, and withdraws into silence whenever the limits are reached. What he wrote to Lavater from Switzerland in October 1779 (when he was thirty years old, and famous)—'My destiny is entirely hidden from men; they can neither see nor hear anything of it'—can be set beside what he wrote a week before his death: 'Our best convictions cannot be translated into words. Language is not good for everything.'

Outside Germany, there are further difficulties attaching to the necessarily perilous task of giving a brief account of Goethe. It is not possible to make allusions which take for granted a knowledge in the English reader of the essential facts and the principal texts. Such knowledge as there is of the great works—or of lyrics like 'Knowst Thou the Land?'—is of little help. *Faust* suggests merely a seduction story, *Werther* a piece of romantic moonshine. But a reader who has been familiar with some particular verse since his school-days may naturally be surprised not to find it here. And there will doubtless be even more dissatisfaction amongst those who, having read more, fail to recognize here any exact reproduction of their own memories. Both may rest assured that the author is even more conscious of the gaps.

Anthologies are barbarous, demanding sacrificial selection. Since Goethe provides something on everything, let us turn to him for some consoling comment. He records in his memoirs that he first encountered Shakespeare quite early in the form of a collection of quotations; and he adds that whatever may be said against such compilations, they nevertheless possess considerable advantages, since it is not always possible for us to embark on a complete work.

It is, furthermore, disgraceful to present a poet in translation.

But here again there is a reassuring text: 'I hold both rhythm and rhyme in honor; by them alone poetry becomes poetry. But what produces a really deep and penetrating effect, what is the really formative and fertilizing element, is what remains of a poet when he is translated into prose.'

We cannot, alas, altogether agree with him as regards lyric poetry, which is most especially his own.

There are, however, plenty of English readers who are not German experts, and for those who do not know Goethe, something, however little, is better than nothing.

From a picture by Georg Oswald May (1779).

Frankfurt on Main, seen from the West (J. J. Koller, 1777.)

II. The Germany of Goethe's Birth

'At noon on the 28th of August, on the stroke of twelve, I came into the world at Frankfurt-on-Main.'

The imperial city of Frankfurt, with rights equal to those of princes, was subordinate only to the supreme sovereign himself, and those who administered it held the title of imperial counsellors. Such was Goethe's father, Johann Caspar (he held the title without fulfilling its functions), and his maternal grandfather, Johann Wolfgang Textor, principal magistrate of the city.

As a matter of fact, the Holy Roman Empire of the German Nation was by now chiefly a glorious memory. It had never recovered from the blow dealt it by the Treaty of Westphalia. Whereas the kings of Europe had quelled their barons and created a unity centered on the throne, the great body of Germany was tending to fall apart. The three hundred and forty-odd German princes, each in possession of his own territorial sovereignty, tried to justify their existence by improved administration or, more frequently, played at royalty with a display of luxury out of all proportion to their importance.

Vienna was finding itself confronted by another power, and a very dangerous one: Protestant Prussia, in opposition to Catholic and traditionalist Austria. In 1740, the year of Maria Theresa's accession, Frederick II came to the throne, inheriting from the Sergeant-Major King his father an army which was not to be allowed to rust in idleness.

The citizens of Frankfurt had more reason than most Germans to feel the proximity of their Emperors. They saw them in person at their coronation, which had, since 1356, taken place within their walls. On that day, all foreigners were severely excluded and the Jews confined to their ghetto. There is a legendary atmosphere surrounding the memory of these ceremonies. They connect Goethe as a child with the beauty of Maria Theresa and her love for Francis of Lorraine, her husband, which she manifested in the very midst of the ceremony of his coronation as Emperor in 1745.

Yet even in this imperial city Frederick II's early victories were watched with sympathy. On the 29th of August 1756, the day after young Johann Wolfgang's seventh birthday, the King of Prussia having just invaded Saxony, Counsellor Goethe offered prayers for his success, whereas the Textor grandparents sided with their lawful sovereign. The peace of the family was disturbed by these differences of opinion, and the women tried in vain to restore it. The child was thrown into some confusion of mind by the critical attacks made on the hero his father so admired.

Despite the hostility of the late Frederick William I towards all foreign frivolities, and despite the variations in Viennese policy which made Louis XV his enemy from 1756 onwards, all Frederick II's sympathies were reserved for French culture: German was a language fit only for horses. And possibly for God, if you happened to believe in Him. What writer of his own land could compare, in the sovereign's eyes, with those of France, the land of 'enlightenment' *par excellence*, the enemy of 'superstition'? *L'Esprit des Lois* appeared in 1748. Diderot and d'Alembert began the publication of the *Encyclopédie* in 1751. After his three years at the Prussian court, which he left in 1753, Voltaire and the King cordially detested each other, but Frederick continued to admire him as a philosophical mind. They resumed their correspondence in 1757, and on the 24th of July 1775 the King wrote: 'We must wait for nature to bring forth men of true genius... The soil which produced one Leibniz may produce others. I shall not see the great days of my country, but I foresee their possibility... As for myself, it is my consolation that I have lived in the century of Voltaire; it is enough.'

Now, 1775 was the year of publication of *Werther* and Goethe's earliest plays. Which meant that those 'abominable things of Shakespeare's... fit for the savages of Canada' had brought to light a German author with sufficient bad taste to produce a 'detestable imitation' of them. And what was worse, the public was 'enthusiastically demanding a repetition of these disgusting platitudes.' *Fredericus dixit.*

Frederick II, by Menzel.

It is one of the ironies of history that it was Frederick himself, by awakening national feeling through his feats of arms, who encouraged this German literature which he did not wish even to hear discussed.

At the time of Goethe's birth this was a development which was only just beginning. The prestige of the Sun King still shone over Germany. The princes overwhelmed their subjects with taxes in order to build for themselves miniature Versailles. At Leipzig, the capital of good taste, Gottsched dominated the theatre with an endless succession of translations or poor imitations of French classics, until Lessing arose to silence his pretensions.

The time was still far distant when Germany was to have poets of her own who could rival the courts of Europe. As for the past, the names of *minnesang* and its sweetest singer, Walther von der Vogelweide, or of Godfrey of Strasbourg and his *Tristan*, or Wolfram von Eschenbach and his *Parsifal*, were all but forgotten. Equally forgotten was the popular epic, with its straightforward heroes—Siegfried, Kriemhild, the Nibelungen—and its ferocity and bloodshed. And the Rhineland mystics of the thirteenth and fourteenth centuries, whose light had once gone forth through Christendom, slept equally undisturbed in the dust of their manuscripts.

The end of the Middle Ages, wasted by war, famine and plague, was productive of little in the way of literature. Faint memory remained of the Strasbourg satirist Sebastian Brand, or of that learned mystic, Cardinal Nicholas of Cusa. Even humanism bequeathed no more than a few folios. Only one poet of the sixteenth century kept his popularity—the shoemaker-master-singer, Hans Sachs.

Luther split Europe in two and built a wall which for centuries hid from Germany her medieval past. In return, he gave her linguistic unity through his translation of the Bible into the Saxon dialect, lying midway between north and south. After him, that uninterrupted succession of tragedies which forms the substance of German history continued on its way. Another thirty years of war, famine and plague. There is little thought of reading or writing in a country which is totally ravaged and has lost more than a third of its population, except of works which reflect and express its misery, like Grimmelshausen's *Simplicissimus*.

The treaties of Westphalia mutilated Germany in her soul as well as in her territory. In the first quarter of the eighteenth century she could name only one man with a European reputation —one who found grace even in the eyes of Frederick II: Leibniz (1646-1716); but to make himself intelligible to the civilized world he found he had to write in French and Latin. In the second quarter, she suddenly showed the full measure of her musical genius: in Bach (1685-1750) and Handel (1685-1759). Then

14

followed Gluck (1714-87), Haydn (1732-1809), Mozart (1756-91) and Beethoven (1770-1827).

In literature, the first great works were not to appear until the third quarter of the century.

During the same period that he was hymning Christ in *The Messiah*, Klopstock (1724-1803) was pouring out the lyricism of his *Odes*, in praise of God and nature and his native land, of love and of friendship. 'Klopstock...' says Lotte to Werther on the day they first meet, as she gazes with emotion upon the spectacle of nature after a storm. In contrast to him there is Wieland (1733-1813), delighting elegant society with his pleasant satires, the poems and novels of a mind disporting itself à la Voltaire.

"Klopstock!" (*Engraving by Tony Johannot for* Werther, *1844*).

Lessing (1729-81), almost the incarnation of the age of enlighten-ment in Germany, wages war against practically everybody in his efforts to destroy the influence of France, while Winckelmann (1717-68) proposes Greek art as the standard of beauty.

From 1770 onwards Kant (1724-1804) was constructing and promulgating his philosophy at Königsberg. And another native of East Prussia, Herder (1744-1803) had begun with passionate ardor to expound his theories on popular poetry and his demands for spontaneity in art. The day was not far distant when circum-stances were to take him to Strasbourg to open Goethe's eyes to himself.

As Goethe emphasized in his memoirs, all these great prede-cessors left some mark on him. He even rescued a certain number of others from oblivion, who, happening to cross his path, obtained the honor of playing some part, however brief, in relation to him. All the great currents of his period find their way into his work. He assimilates and transcends them all. He dominates the end of the eighteenth century and the first third of the following one. He can be compared only with the great men of the Renaissance, Leonardo da Vinci or Michelangelo, for the width of his knowledge and the universality and power of his genius. No work of man ever bore the inscription *Homo sum* on its frontispiece with more aptitude and splendor than his. The modern age has found in Goethe its most perfect representative, and if the iron age upon which we are now entering cannot see him with quite the same eyes as his contemporaries, yet he still possesses riches enough to offer something beneficial to anyone willing to approach him.

Goethe wrote this line from Horace in a theological student's album. He was then fifteen years old.

Mors ultima linea rerum.

Trajecti Francorum
ad Moenum.
D. IV Aug. MDCCLXIV

Haecce, in sui sem-
piternam memori-
am, huic inscribere
voluit libello

Goethe

JOHANN CASPAR GOETHE
AND KATHARINA ELISABETH TEXTOR
by J. P. Melchior (1779).

III. Frankfurt:
August 28th 1749 to October 1765

Family – Home – Education – The French Occupation – First Essays – First Love: Gretchen.

Goethe's great-grandfather was a smith, his grandfather a master tailor and afterwards an innkeeper. The latter's son, Johann Caspar Goethe, was thirty-eight when, on the 20th of August 1748, he married Katharine Elisabeth Textor, born at Frankfurt on the 19th of February 1731 of a family of lawyers.

There was less difference in age (and in other ways) between the young wife and her two first children, Johann Wolfgang (28th of August 1749) and Cornelie (7th of December 1750), than between her and her pedantic old husband. There was always a strong bond of affection and mutual confidence between Goethe and his sister. Five more children quickly followed, but they died in infancy.

Goethe summed up in four much-quoted lines what he thought he owed to each of his parents: to his father, gravity of conduct; to his mother, cheerfulness, and delight in the telling of tales.

All that he says of his father, though objective in form and respectful in tone, contains a certain quiet bitterness. He could

hardly manage to forgive him either the strictness of his education or, still less the pedagogic spirit and the near-mania for collecting, arranging and classifying which he believed he had inherited from him. 'My hypochondriac, finicky father... with his dry, serious mind...'

Of his mother, on the other hand, he says that she was 'very lively and high-spirited... able to bear anything except worry... always gay and good-humored, and desirous that others should be the same.' Contemporary accounts of this charming woman confirm her son's judgment.

The family shared with Goethe's paternal grandmother a house in the street called the Deers' Ditch. It was a rather dark and gloomy building until the extensive alterations made in 1755, but Goethe as an old man remembered his childhood impressions of it with great affection:

On the second floor there was a room called the garden room, because a few plants had been put in the window with the idea of compensating for the lack of a garden. As I grew older, it came to be my favorite place for sitting in and being not exactly sad, but melancholy.... It was there that I usually learnt my lessons in summer, waited for thunderstorms to pass over, and gazed, as I never could do enough, at the setting sun, which the windows directly faced.... This awakened

Goethe's mother.

The house where Goethe was born, before the alterations of 1755.

The house in the Deers' Ditch after the alterations of 1755.

in me quite early a feeling of loneliness from which flowed a sense of yearning; this, corresponding as it did to a certain foreboding solemnity which nature had given me, soon manifested its influence in me, as it did even more clearly at a later date.

Of his brief schooldays, Goethe remembered the master's cane and the brutal bullying of some of the boys. His sufferings at that time gave him the opportunity of practicing stoicism 'as seriously as a small boy can.'

The ragging, and the infectious diseases caught at school, made his father decide to entrust his children to tutors. Johann Wolfgang now learnt Latin, Greek, Italian, English, music and drawing, the latter remaining for many years one of his favorite pursuits. He even embarked on Yiddish and Hebrew. For exercise, he had skating, fencing, riding and dancing. The Counsellor's educational system had at least the merit of eclecticism. Moreover it was he who aroused his son's longing for Italy, in which he had spent a considerable time:

Inside the house, the thing which most held my eyes was a set of pictures of Rome, with which my father had adorned the entrance-hall.... These forms made a deep impression on me....

The child's interest in the theatre was early aroused by the puppet-plays performed by his grandmother. He did plenty of reading: old folk-tales—*Melusine, The Four Sons of Aymon, Till Eulenspiegel, Fortunatus*—and also *Robinson Crusoe*, Fénelon's *Télémaque*, and the Bible in a handsome edition illustrated with engravings.

His father was a rationalist, contemporary style, though preserving a respect for Protestantism in its traditional form. His mother's piety was more sincere. The Lisbon earthquake came in 1755 to confound the optimism of the Age of Enlightenment. Its prolonged repercussions in the public mind dealt a first blow to the child's faith:

God, the creator and sustainer of heaven and earth, who had been presented to him as so wise and merciful in the expounding of the first article of the creed, in delivering the just and the unjust to a like destruction had shown Himself to be in no way fatherly. His young mind strove in vain to recover from this impression; it was all the more impossible, in that even wise and learned people were unable to agree on the way in which such a phenomenon ought to be regarded.

It would be a mistake to think of young Johann Wolfgang as a boy entirely devoted to his studies, his sole inclination solitary meditation on moral problems. Extremes were already meeting in him, and his general curiosity took other forms besides that of a taste for reading. He explored the old streets of the town, admiring the bridge over the Main, the famous town hall—the Römer—and the fine old houses. Delight in the past is one of the early characteristics stressed in the memoirs, but there were more

Frankfurt Town Hall.

positive distractions, too, to be found in the town's great fairs with all their motley excitement.

The official position of his Textor grandfather gave him a glimpse of the affairs of the city. Fifty years later he was able to produce portraits of the citizens of Frankfurt of that time which would have been drawn with a less sure touch if his great powers of observation had not already been awakened in his childhood. His father often sent him with messages to the workmen he

*The Comte
de Thoranc.*

employed. 'Thus I was strengthened in my sense of the equality if not of all men at least of all human conditions; it seemed to me that existence itself was the primary matter, and everything else fortuitous and unimportant.'

Seventeen fifty-six saw the beginning of the Seven Years' War. In 1759 the French entered Frankfurt. The big house in the Deers' Ditch had to open its doors to the Comte de Thoranc. He was the *lieutenant du roi*, i.e., a high police-official; but he was, for all that, polished, courtly, and a patron of the arts. This was no help in recommending him to Counsellor Goethe, who grew more morose and recalcitrant than ever. Matters almost took a tragic turn on the day of the Battle of Bergen when, in the Comte's presence, Herr Goethe loudly cursed the victorious French. His young wife, true to her own nature, made the best of the situation. As for the children, they were delighted to have the house turned upside down. The little boy acquired a love for the French language which he never lost. His theatrical interests also profited from the French occupation:

Many of the words were familiar to me from Latin; Italian gave an introduction to still more. So, in a short time I had picked up so much from servants, soldiers, sentries and visitors that, if I could not join in conversation, at least I could understand individual questions and answers. But all this was little in comparison with the blessing of the theatre. 'I had been given a free ticket by my grandfather, and I used it every day, in defiance of my father and with my mother's connivance. So there I sat in the pit with a foreign stage in front of me paying all the more attention, to movement, mime and style of enunciation because I understood little or nothing of what they were saying up there and so had to find my entertainments entirely in the play of gesture and intonation . . . Not long afterwards I seized on the copy of Racine which I found in my father's library and declaimed the plays in theatrical style . . . with great animation,

24

but still without being able to understand the whole of any one speech.
Moreover, I learned whole passages by heart and recited them
like a well-trained parrot . . .

'I began writing verses in my tenth year...'

Like his Greek and Latin exercises of the same period, Goethe's
youthful compliments addressed to his grandparents give evidence
of nothing beyond extreme facility. He kept a prose version of
the story of Joseph, and those he considered best of the verses,
together making up one good-sized quarto manuscript, which he
later consigned to the flames. All that remains of these first efforts
is a poem written to order in 1765, *The Descent of Jesus Christ*
into Hell—sixteen ten-line stanzas of frigid pomposity, relieved
here and there by something more dynamic.

But he found that the boys he knew also wrote poems, which
they thought good while he considered them bad. Wasn't he,
then, deluding himself about his own standard? 'I was much
troubled about this for a long while, for there was no possibility
of my discovering any external evidence of the truth.'

As for me, I certainly had in mind to produce something extra-
ordinary; but in what it was to consist was by no means clear to me.
But, as we are always readier to think of the reward for which we
hope than of the service which we are to render, I will not deny that
whenever I thought about a joy that would be worth having it always
seemed most alluring when it appeared in the form of the laurel
crown men weave to adorn a poet.

He was, then, a born poet. And, almost to the same degree, a
born lover. The lover in him inspired the poet. Or was it rather
that love was never more than a marvelous and ever-fresh occasion
of song to the poet, which he was always ready to seize? We
shall leave the critics to their endless discussion of the point. What
is certain is that whenever conflict arose between love and his
vocation as a poet it was love that was sacrificed, in virtue of a
higher obligation involving the very law of his being, his daemon.

We are anticipating. However, Johann Wolfgang had already
(being between ten and thirteen years old) met the daughter of
one of the actresses in the wings of the French theatre, and felt
a stirring of the heart. He always made a point of bringing her
some little present. She thanked him prettily and paid no further
attention to him. There is no drama here, but tragedy was not
far off.

In about his fifteenth year a friend introduced him into somewhat doubtful society. The boys in question asked him to write

a passionate love-letter in verse in order to mystify a certain love-sick young man. One evening when he was having dinner with them a girl came in of 'incredible beauty'—a relative of theirs, who had come instead of the maid, who was ill. She had 'frank, steady eyes,' a 'darling mouth,' a 'charming' profile. 'Everything about her was exquisite.' Her name was Gretchen.

Her image pursued him everywhere. 'This was the first abiding impression which any feminine creature had made upon me...' It being impossible for him to meet her at her own home, he went to church to see her, never taking his eyes off her throughout the whole long service. 'When we came out I was not bold enough to speak to her, still less to accompany her; it was bliss enough that she seemed to notice me and to answer my bow with a nod.'

We have glimpses of her in one or two scenes which have been popularized by all the arts. 'Gretchen was sitting in the window spinning...' 'Gretchen was standing in front of the mirror putting on her hat' (for want of Mephistopheles' jewels).

In order to go on meeting his love the boy kept up his part in the practical joke, though he strongly disliked it. One day when he had read her a page of the passionate stuff he had written, Gretchen picked up the pen and signed it, but she would not give him so much as a kiss. 'I pressed my face into her hands and hurried away. In all my life I have never been in such a turmoil.'

'Through the image of this girl and my attachment to her a new world of beauty and sublimity had risen up before me...' Thus Gretchen provided the first sketch of that vision of the Eternal Feminine drawing man up to the heights of which the poet was to write in his old age in the last lines of *Faust*.

The excitement in the town over the approaching coronation gave him the chance of seeing her more often in the evenings. The idyll progressed to an accompaniment of crowd-noises. The great day itself, April 3rd, 1764, he spent with her and his friends. 'When I had seen Gretchen to her door she kissed me on the forehead. This was the first and last time she granted me such a favor; for alas, I was never to see her again.'

One of the counsellors, and a friend of the family, called at his parents' house next day and broke it to them that their son's friends were involved in a complicated case of forged papers. His father was, naturally, beside himself. Johann Wolfgang was subjected to close interrogation:

I could not deny that I had come home late several nights, that I had got hold of a key to the house, that I had more than once been

26

seen with persons of low station and suspicious appearance in places of entertainment, and that there were girls mixed up with it all; in short, it seemed that everything was discovered except the names.

In his despair he half thought of suicide. In imagination he saw his friends, and Gretchen above all, 'imprisoned, interrogated, punished, disgraced.' He fell ill. To calm him, he was promised that the guilty parties would be leniently treated. Gretchen was sent home to the country.

There are, as a matter of fact, points which are not absolutely clear about this story, which is told us only by Goethe himself. Thanks, no doubt, to his Textor grandfather, the documents of the trial have disappeared. We may observe that at about the same time Goethe applied for admission to a 'secret society' of young people, and one of the members advised against accepting him 'because of his vices.' Was the reputation of his friends not above reproach? Had he himself suspected nothing?

After this crisis he was given a mentor—friend and guardian in one. This man told him one day what Gretchen had said about him at the trial: 'I cannot deny that I have often seen him, and with great pleasure; but I always regarded him as a child, and my affection for him was purely sisterly.'

This was such a blow to his love and pride that he thought himself cured of his passion on the spot. He would no longer allow Gretchen anything of charm or innocence. But her image still haunted him and he was unhappy:

My wanderings through the streets had come to an end; like other people, I went only where I had to. I never went to Gretchen's part of the town again, nor even anywhere near it. I gradually began to be disgusted by these old walls and towers of mine, and to dislike the whole plan of the town. Everything which had once impressed me as so venerable now appeared only in distorted images.

This is from the sixth book of the memoirs. His childhood was over.

*A family portrait in the fashionable pastoral convention,
by Seekatz (Frankfurt 1762).*

IV. Leipzig:
October 1765 to August 1768

The University – Annette – Behrisch-
Mephisto – Anacreontism – The first
fragments of the 'great confession.'

Johann Caspar Goethe had decided, contrary to the boy's own wish, that his son should study law at Leipzig. Goethe would have preferred Göttingen, and shuddered at the thought that he might find himself condemned to an existence like his father's. He arrived at Leipzig, after a moderately exciting journey, in October 1765, in the middle of the fair, which was reminiscent of his own native town. On the 19th he enrolled in the University, which, with its five-hundred-odd students, was one of the most heavily attended centers of learning of the period.

Armed with his letters of introduction he went to see his future masters, and sent an account of these visits to the old gentleman in Frankfurt, who will have been, no doubt, quite unaware of any irony in the tone:

I do nothing now but work away at Latin.—One word more!
You cannot think what a splendid thing a professor is. I am simply
captivated by having seen some of them in all their glory: nil istis
splendidius, gravius, ac honoratius.

However, he confesses to his friend Riese a little later that he is dissipating himself in 'social gatherings, concerts, plays, receptions, dinners, walks,' and that he is very well pleased with the life he is living—which does not hinder him from lavishing tutorial admonitions, in English and French, on Cornelie.

Disillusionment was swift. He was teased for his Frankfurt accent and his good, hard-wearing, ill-cut clothes. This latter handicap, at least, was quickly overcome. He applied himself zealously to his lectures at the start, but was soon weary of them:

In the matter of logic, it seemed very odd to me that I was expected to take the mental operations which I had been performing with the greatest ease from my youth upwards and worry them to pieces, isolate them and so to speak destroy them in order to learn the right way to use them.

As we shall find Mephistopheles saying to the student:

And so, my dear friend, I commend you first of all to the Collegium Logicum. That's where they'll give your mind a good drilling, and

lace it into Spanish boots, so that it can tiptoe down the highroad of thought more circumspectly henceforward, and not go criss-crossing and jack-o'-lanterning all over the place.

Goethe had no liking for Gottsched and his perruque; and little more for Gellert, poet and professor, whose students loved to submit their literary productions to him. Did he still believe in himself? 'Since coming to Leipzig, I have learnt that you have to be something great if you are to be anything at all. And I have likewise recovered from the folly of thinking myself a poet.' (To

Gellert, by Graff (1769).

Cornelie, in French, on the 27th of September 1766.) 'Since November I have written about fifteen poems, not particularly long or important. I can't show a single one of them to Gellert, for I know his current views on poetry. They must let me go my own way; if I do have genius I shall become a poet whether anyone improves me or not; if I haven't, no criticism will do me any good.' (To Cornelie, in German, 11th of May 1767.)

From good society, which had already much disappointed him, he now became further detached by a love affair. His friend and future brother-in-law Schlosser came to Leipzig at Easter, 1766, and introduced him to the boarding-house kept by the Schönkopf family; Goethe went to live there. The daughter of the house was called Kätchen or Annette. A few days later Goethe declared his love for her.

It was a student's affair, a sensual passion for a girl a little older than himself, sweet-tempered and by no means strait-laced, though with a certain respect for appearances. But at this time Goethe had also got to know Behrisch, one of the models for Mephistopheles; eleven years his senior, a pedant, a rake and a cynic. Auerbach's wine-cellar, where he took his young friend, was to find its way into *Faust*. In his efforts to measure up to his new master, Goethe began drinking and chasing after women, with an affectation of libertinism for which he laughed at himself:

Do you know me in this style, Behrisch? The true ladykiller style. And that style and myself together! It's ridiculous. But, to make no bones about it, I'd already be fit to ... how the devil do I put it? ... a girl. In short, Monsieur, all you can possibly look for from the most docile and attentive of your pupils... (7th November 1767).

He was, be it noted, just eighteen years old.

Behrisch was a better counsellor where poetry was concerned. From amongst Goethe's recent work he selected twelve pieces, and these, as carefully copied by him, constitute the 'Book of Annette.' They were not recovered, in their original form, until 1895. They display skill, grace, and considerable eroticism, while the 'Elegy on the Death of my Friend's Brother' strikes a note which is already almost authentic Goethe. His readers in the case of this first selection were 'twelve men and two women.' 'That's the sum total of my public,' he wrote to Cornelie. 'I don't like fuss.'

His three odes to Behrisch are in the Klopstock tradition. Other poems of this period, set to music in the Breitkopf circle, where he was a visitor, already evoke something of the atmosphere and, barring the anacreontic conceits, something of the incantatory power which his lyric poetry was to have:

NIGHT

Gladly do I leave the cottage
That's my fair one's dwelling-place,
And with footsteps soft I wander
Through the forest's emptiness.

Through the oak-trees' night breaks Luna,
Zephyrs heralding her path,
And the birches, bowing, strew
Before her sweetest incense-breath.

Thrilling awe, which makes the heart
Awake to feeling, melts the soul,
Wanders through the leafy coolness.
Sweet and lovely is the night!
Joy and pleasure past conceiving!
Yet, o Heaven, I'd willingly
Leave thee of thy nights a thousand
Would my girl give one to me.[1]

Meanwhile, however, his affair with Annette had turned to storm and tempest. Irritated by his inability to come to any conclusion about his own talent, and dissatisfied with Leipzig and with himself, he turned against her, inflicting a terrible series of jealous scenes on her. 'She bore it for a while with an incredible patience which I was cruel enough to try to its utmost limits. But, to my shame and despair, I was forced to realize at last that I had alienated her affection...' There had never been any question of marriage between them: 'If she can find a good husband, and live happily without me, how happy I shall be!'

But Goethe would not be Goethe if he did not always leave something of himself behind in any passionate adventure which befell him. His affair with Annette inspired two comedies, *Die Laune des Verliebten* (*The Lover's Whim*) and *Die Mitschuldigen* (*Accomplices*) which, as he tells us, were the first fragments of his 'great confession.'

One day in August 1768 he began to cough blood; a symptom of a somewhat mysterious illness which has provided matter for endless speculation and which, at the time, put his life in danger. He now began his long series of sudden departures, leaving Leipzig without any farewell to the Schönkopfs. As soon as his condition allowed—it was actually his birthday, the 28th August 1768—he got into a hired carriage and arrived at Frankfurt on the 1st September, 'like a castaway.'

---

[1] I have given the youthful poems in their original versions, not in the revised forms in which Goethe afterwards included them in the various editions of his works. (J. A.-H.)

V. Frankfurt:
September 1768 to March 1770

Illness – A religious crisis – Fräulein von Klettenberg – Alchemy and pietism – Striving for faith.

'My soul is quiet, without desire or pain or joy or memory,' he wrote on the eighth of September 1768. But a few lines further on: 'My love, that unhappy passion which cost me far, far more than I can ever forget, is sunken and buried in the depths of my memory.'

'Tell me, can anything sadder than this be known? To be old in body and young in years, half sick and half well?' (6th November 1768). The long letter with these lines in it was sent to Friederike Oeser, a girl in Leipzig whose tranquil friendship had sometimes restored his soul to peace amid the turmoil he suffered over Annette. Goethe had had drawing lessons from her father, who was the director of the Academy of Fine Arts. So the castaway had salvaged something from the wreck: the influence of this man, of Wieland and of Shakespeare, as he was to record when drawing up his balance-sheet for this period.

During his absence the situation in his family had not improved. Counsellor Goethe's faults had grown to an intolerable degree, and he was now in a state of fury at seeing his son's years of study at Leipzig coming to such a conclusion.

Frau Goethe had taken refuge in Pietism. Her particular friend in these circles was a Fräulein von Klettenberg whom Goethe was to portray as the 'beautiful soul' in *Wilhelm Meister*, and, even more vividly, in his memoirs. She was forty-five; natural and warm-hearted. 'She looked on her illness as a necessary element in her transitory earthly existence; she suffered with the utmost patience, and during the intervening periods when she had no pain she was animated and ready to talk.'

Religion was in Goethe's soul. He had a deep sense of the sacred and a recognition of a reality higher than man. He was to preserve throughout his life his attachment to the Bible, 'for it was to it practically alone that I owed my moral formation.' But he had been disappointed as a child by the inadequacy of the old man who had given him religious instruction, and by the poverty of the sacramental life as experienced in Protestantism: a confession powerless to restore peace of soul and a Lord's Supper of which you could never be sure of being worthy. 'I was so tormented by this dreary scruple, and the supposedly adequate remedy I was offered seemed so bare and so feeble as only to lend my nightmare vision a more terrible aspect; as soon as I arrived at Leipzig I set about detaching myself completely from all ties with the Church.'

But now illness was forcing him back on himself, and he surrendered to the guidance of Fräulein von Klettenberg:

My restlessness and impatience, my strivings and seekings and probings and moods and instabilities were all interpreted by her in her own way. Nor did she conceal her conviction from me, but assured me without any embarrassment that it was all the result of my not being reconciled to God. Now I had believed, from my youth upwards, that I was on quite good terms with my God; indeed, I even had it in mind, on the basis of various experiences of mine, that He might be rather in arrears where I was concerned: I had the temerity to think that I had something to forgive Him. The basis of this conceit was my own limitless good will; He should, it seemed to me, have come to its aid rather better than He had. It may easily be conceived how often my friend and I disputed over this...

The letters of this period sound a rather different note. On the 9th of November 1768 he writes to his friend Langer, in French: 'You were the first man in this world to preach the true Gospel to me, and if God gives me the grace to make me a Christian, it is to you that I shall owe the first germ of it. God bless you for that.'

And on the 24th, in German this time:

And for all that, I am not yet a Christian; but then, does it lie within my powers as a man to make myself one? I have the best of hopes. This hot head of mine, and my mind, and my efforts and hopes—which are pretty well founded—of becoming a good writer in time arę, as I must frankly state, the principal obstacles at this moment to my thorough conversion, and to a really serious and eager response to the beckonings of grace. As you see, I am speaking unreservedly; it is very largely a misplaced spark of self-respect which is still too strong and, I fear, is going to grow stronger.

Because he was in reaction against the rationalism and dogmatic discussions of the official Church, the wholly affective Christianity of Pietism had the power of appealing to his sensibility; but the low rating given in these circles to intellectual values contributed, no doubt, to setting up this barrier to his 'conversion.'

He was suffering from an ulcer of the throat and from serious digestive troubles. The doctor who was attending him was in possession of a 'universal remedy,' of which the secret could be acquired by the perusal of certain books of a mystical and chemical-alchemical character. Through Fräulein von Klettenberg, who had already secretly read Welling's *Opus Mago Cabbalisticum*, her young pupil was 'inoculated with this disease.' Together they plunged into the reading of all kinds of books 'whose lineal descent can be traced back to the Neo-platonist school'—Paracalsus, Basilius Valentinus, Van Helmont, Starckey and others. In his memoirs he treats them with a certain scepticism. Did he take them perfectly seriously at the time?

One day in December 1768 he underwent a violent crisis; his anxious mother, fearing the worst, implored the doctor to employ his 'remedy.' It was followed by an amelioration.

Goethe continued to move in Pietist circles and took part, in his own home, in their religious services:

I am young, and I am walking a path which will certainly lead me out of the labyrinth. Could someone but promise me: The light will shine upon you always as it does now, and you will never again go astray! But why such anxieties? This weakness of faith still persists. Peter was such another as we are, an upright man but for his cowardice. If he had firmly believed that Jesus had power over heaven, earth and sea he would have walked on the sea dry-shod; it was his doubt which made him sink. You know, Langer, ours is a strange case. The Savior has seized me at last; I seemed to Him to be running overlong and overfast; He has taken me by the hair. And He is certainly after you too, and I shall see Him catch you, only I cannot say in what way it will be. I sometimes feel entirely at peace about this; sometimes when I am quiet, completely quiet, and I can feel all the good which has been flowing over me from the eternal source. Even if we go wandering a long while yet, you and I, we shall reach the goal. (17th January 1769.)

Despite his relapses, his physical cure was becoming manifest. By the spring, he was convalescent and back in his own dear attic room, which he turned into a laboratory for the practice of chemistry, tinged with alchemy according to the directions of the ancient authors he was reading. These experiments were the prelude to his scientific work at Weimar. They were also to leave their mark on many of the scenes in *Faust*.

This Frankfurt period constitutes an eighteen-month interval, a time of meditation and spiritual exploration, one of the most hidden periods of Goethe's life. He reached the peak of his religious mysticism. He was deeply impressed by Arnold's 'History of the Church and the Heretics' (published in Frankfurt in 1688-93), and as he had heard it said that in the end each man really has his own religion, he set about the construction of one. So Book VIII of the memoirs here becomes a cosmogony inspired by Platonism, the Cabal and alchemy; but in elaborating this in 1811 Goethe inserted certain ideas which only came to him later on.

In the spring of 1770 I felt that not only my health but also my youthful good spirits were restored, and I longed once more to be out of my father's house.

He had to finish his legal studies. This time it was Strasbourg that he chose—Strasbourg, belonging to France, in 'beautiful Alsace,' which he already loved by anticipation, lying on the frontier between the Germanic and Latin cultures.

His departure was hastened by a scene with his father. He left by coach and arrived at Strasbourg at the end of March.

Drawing of himself by Goethe,
in his attic in Frankfurt.

View of Strasbourg, from an engraving of 1775.

VI. Strasbourg:
April 1770 to August 1771

The cathedral – Herder – Sturm und Drang – Sesenheim and Friederike Brion – The new lyricism – Departure – Epilogue.

'*I am a student once more, and I have now, thank God, all the health I need and high spirits in plenty.*' (12th April 1770.)

He strove to overcome his morbid sensitivity—to conquer his horror of noise, his tendency to vertigo, and the repugnance he felt at the sight of physical ills. He walked beside marching troops, placing himself beside the drums; he climbed alone to the top of the cathedral, and paid frequent visits to a clinic so as to overcome his disgusted reactions and at the same time to learn anatomy.

His pious aspirations had faded rapidly away: 'My intercourse with pious people in this place is not very persistent. . . . They are so heartily boring, when they get started, that my lively spirits couldn't bear it.' (To Fräulein von Klettenberg, 26th August 1770.)

Strasbourg's first revelation to him was its cathedral:

How often I returned to contemplate its grandeur and majesty from every side, at every distance, in every sort of light! . . . How

39

freshly it shone before me in the light morning mists; and with what joy I would stretch out my arms to it and see all the great harmonious masses of it, living in each of their innumerable subdivisions, just as, in the works of eternal nature, everything has its form·and everything is orientated towards the whole, down to the least and smallest of fibers. How lightly that great edifice, with its vast and solid foundations, soared into the air! How delicate it was in its open tracery, yet how eternally permanent!

Herder, by Graff.

The second event of his time in Strasbourg was his meeting with Herder: a momentous event in Goethe's life and in the history of German literature.

Herder was a native of Königsberg. He had come to Strasbourg as traveling-companion to a prince, and stayed there for treatment for his eyes. He was five years older than Goethe and had already written much, especially on the subjects of literature and language.

I began to know poetry from an entirely different aspect, in an entirely different sense from hitherto—and one which was very much to my taste. Hebrew poetry, which he, following Lowth, expounded with great understanding, folk-poetry—he drove us to explore Alsace for traditional forms of it—and the poetic form taken by the most ancient documents, all bore witness to the truth that poetry is a gift to the world and its peoples, not a private heirloom of a few refined, cultured people.... If I am to describe the fullness of those few weeks which we spent together, I may say that everything which Herder afterwards gradually developed was indicated then, as though in the bud, and that I was therefore in the happy position of seeing everything which I had hitherto thought, learnt and made my own being given its completion, linked up with something higher, and broadened.... It was he who first introduced me to Hamann's writings, to which he attached a very considerable value.

Hamann was 'the wizard of the north': anti-rationalist, pietist, sententious, sybilline. It was thanks to Herder, too, that Goethe got to know the poems of Ossian and translated them, that he made a closer study of the Greeks and began to admire Shakespeare with increased fervor.

Herder was surrounded by a circle of young men—Klinger, Lenz, H. L. Wagner—who made his ideas their watchwords and, through him, those of Rousseau and Hamann: the return to nature, the primacy of feeling, the cult of genius. The powerful personality, the 'titan,' obeys his own intuition, without reference to moral and social rules, asserting himself against his environment, which he dominates by his own mind and heart. It was Goethe who gave this movement its letters-patent. They called it *Sturm und Drang*, after the title of one of Klinger's plays: *Sturm* —storm in both the meteorological and military senses; *Drang*— a surge of movement from the deepest instinctual forces in a being.

We come now to the happiest time of Goethe's youth, one of the happiest of his whole life. His fellow-boarder Weyland, a medical student, took him to the parsonage at Sesenheim. Pastor

Brion and his family are reminiscent of the characters in *The Vicar of Wakefield*, which was in vogue at the time. One of the daughters was eighteen years old; her name was Friederike. She used to wear the traditional costume of Alsace.

A short, white, full skirt, with a flounce, not so long as to prevent the prettiest little feet from being visible up to the ankle; a close-fitting white bodice and a black taffeta apron—she was as it were poised on the borderline between peasant-girl and townswoman. Slender and light, she walked as though she had nothing on her, and her neck seemed almost too fragile for the massive golden plaits on her dainty little head. She looked frankly around her with merry blue eyes, and her pretty little turned-up nose took the air as freely as though there were no such thing as care in the whole world; her straw hat was hanging on her arm; and so I had the pleasure, in my very first sight of her, of seeing her and realizing her all at once, in all her grace and loveliness.

Our only knowledge of this idyll is from the memoirs and from one single letter of Goethe's; the rest of the correspondence was destroyed. The one letter was written on the 15th of October 1771, just after their first meeting, and it expresses only timidity and tenderness: 'Strasbourg never seemed so empty to me as it does now.' Happily, it is not a long road to Sesenheim.

WELCOME AND PARTING

My heart beat: Swift to horse! Away!
Wild as a hero to the fight!
Already evening cradled earth,
And on the mountains hung the night.
The oak-tree, in a robe of mist,
Stood like a towering giant there,
Where darkness, with a hundred eyes
Of blackness, from the thicket stared.

The moon from out a hill of cloud
Gazed through the vapor sleepily;
The wind, with softly beating wings,
About my ears breathed eerily.
Night called a thousand monsters forth:
Courage a thousand times was higher.
What burning heat was in my veins,
And, glowing in my heart, what fire!

I saw you, and a gentle gladness
Flowed over me at that sweet view;
All of my heart was at your side
And yours was every breath I drew.
A rosy-colored springtime air
Was all around that lovely face,
And tenderness for me—you gods!
I hoped, but not deserved such grace!

How soon, alas, at morning's sun
It cramped my heart to part again:
What ecstasy was in your kisses!
In your eyes, what bitter pain!
I went, you stood, looked at the ground,
Then after me, with eyes all moist:
And yet what joy to be thus loved!
And, gods, to love, what joy of joys!

His love burst forth with the buds of the year, and his genius
with it. Herder had freed him from Anacreon and the French
conventions of gallantry; he was able to express himself spontaneously. He was twenty; he was in love; it was the world's
first spring.

The parsonage at Sesenheim. Drawing by Goethe, 1770.

MAY DAY

How glorious nature
  Beams on me!
How shines the sun!
  How smiles the mead!

There are blossoms bursting
  From every twig,
And a thousand voices
  Out of the brake,

And dizzy delight
  From every breast.
O earth, o sun!
  O joy, o bliss!

O love, o love!
  So golden fair,
Like morning clouds
  On the hilltops there!

You sovereignly bless
  The fresh-grown field,
In the scent of flowers
  The o'erflowing world.

O maiden, maiden,
  I love you so!
O the look in your eyes!
  You love me so!

Even as the lark
  Loves song and air,
And the flowers of morning
  The breath of heaven.

So I love you
  With my warm heart's blood,
Who give me youth
  And joy, and the mood

> For new singing
> And dancing give.
> Be joyous for ever,
> As you love me indeed!

Love... love...: the word occurs seven times in six verses.

Never had he felt so happy as at Sesenheim in these days of May 1771. And yet...

The most delightful country, people who love me, a whole round of joys. Isn't this the fulfilment of all your childhood dreams? I sometimes ask myself, as I feast my eyes on this horizon of delights. Are not these the enchanted gardens for which you longed? They are, they are! I feel it so, my dear friend, and I feel too that we are not a scrap happier when we have what we desired. O the extras, the extras with which fate weighs down each gift of happiness!' (To his friend Salzmann, from Strasbourg. Written at Sesenheim, 19th of June 1771?)

Was the question of marriage raised? All our records imply that Friederike believed it was to be. But Goethe felt the call of his daemon to greater heights than could be realized through so easy a happiness. He was so young. And what sort of life could there be at his side for a little country girl to whom even Strasbourg felt like a foreign place? On the 6th of August 1771 he passed his examination, and, resorting to what was becoming a familiar pattern of life, returned to his father's house. His rose-in-the-heather was broken indeed, but he himself bore away a secret wound.

> A boy saw a little rose,
> A little rose on the heath;
> It was so young and morning-fair
> Swift he ran to see it near,
> Saw it with great delight.
> Little rose, little rose, little red rose,
> Little rose on the heath.

> Said the boy: 'I'm going to pick you,
> Little rose on the heath.'
> Little rose said: 'I shall prick you,
> So you'll think of me for ever,
> And I will not suffer it.'
> Little rose, little rose, little red rose,
> Little rose on the heath.

> *The boy was rough and wild, and broke*
> *The little rose on the heath.*
> *Little rose fought back and pricked him,*
> *'Woe' and 'alas,' though, were no help:*
> *Still she had to suffer it.*
> > *Little rose, little rose, little red rose,*
> > *Little rose on the heath.*

Friederike's answer to a written farewell tore my heart in two. Here were the very hand, the very mind, the very feelings which had been formed for me and by me. Only now did I feel the loss which she was suffering, and I saw no way to remedy or even to alleviate it. She was utterly present to me; I felt constantly how much I missed her, and the worst of all was that I had to blame myself for my own unhappiness. Gretchen had been taken from me; Annette had deserted me; here, for the first time, it was I who was guilty; I had wounded the most exquisite of hearts in its very depths, and so this time of dreary remorse, void of that refreshing love to which I had grown accustomed, was most painful and indeed intolerable.

... But during this time when I was troubled by distress over Friederike's situation, I turned for help once more, according to my old habit, to the art of poetry. I went on with the poetical confession which I had been making before, in order that, through this penitential self-torment, I might grow worthy of absolution. The two Maries in Goetz von Berlichingen *and* Clavigo, *and the evil part played by their two lovers, may well be the result of these remorseful cogitations.'*

Whereas some of Goethe's finest pages are consecrated to Friederike, the critics have treated her harshly. Not only is she supposed to have let Goethe seduce her but also—a thesis for which bad faith alone can find evidence—to have had numerous lovers after him. All sorts of passions, including even national and religious, have combined to vilify her. Perhaps the figures of Margarethe and her child, deserted by Faust, have played their part in this. We know nothing of their relationship except what Goethe wrote: he says that they used to be left alone together, trusting to Friederike's interior dispositions and to his own honor. His environment here was at a quite different level of conduct from that of the Schönkopf boardinghouse. But even if we are to suppose that youth and love brought them to transgress the limits, it can be plainly felt that his feeling for Friederike was of a totally different quality from his passion for Annette.

On the evening of the 25th I went round by Sesenheim, while the others kept to the direct route. I found a family there, all together, just as I left them eight years ago, and I was given a good and very friendly welcome. Now that I am as pure and calm as air, the atmosphere surrounding good, tranquil people is very welcome to me. The younger daughter of the house loved me once, better than I deserved and better than others upon whom I have expended much in passion and fidelity. I had to leave her at a moment when it almost cost her her life; she made no more than a passing reference to it, in connection with the after-effects of an illness dating from that time. She behaved perfectly charmingly, with the warmest friendliness, from the very moment when I appeared at the door, quite without warning, and we almost bumped into each other. It did me a great deal of good. I should add that she did not try, even by the slightest hint, to awaken anything of my former feeling in my soul. She took me through all the arbors in the garden, and made me sit down and feel at home there. There was a beautiful full moon. I heard all their news.... I found some old songs that I had written, and a carriage which I had painted; we recalled many of the jokes of those good days, and I found that my memory was as fresh among them as if I had been gone a bare six months. Her parents were most cordial. They said that I had got younger. I spent the night there and left next day at sunrise, with friendly faces to bid me farewell; so much so that I can begin once more to think with pleasure of that little corner of the world and, being reconciled with the ghosts of that time, to be at peace with them within myself.
(To Frau von Stein, 25th September 1779).

Lenz, the poet, asked for Friederike's hand after Goethe had left. She refused him and never married. She died in the house of one of her sisters on the 3rd of April 1813, at Messenheim in the Duchy of Baden.

VII. Frankfurt:
August 1771 to May 1772

The Wanderer's Storm-Song – Shakespeare – Plans for Goetz von Berlichingen

He now saw Frankfurt as a 'miserable hole. *Spelunca.* God deliver us from this wretchedness. Amen.'

Yet there was pleasant society available for him even in Frankfurt—acquaintances, old and new, of both sexes. He had contacts in Darmstadt, too, with some 'very cultured' people, amongst whom were Herder's fiancée and Merck—who, with his self-conscious, sardonic bitterness provided another model for Mephisto. It was among them that he spoke of his plans, read whatever he was writing, and received the greatest encouragement.

The unhappiness he was suffering over his love for Friederike and his remorse over her drove him to seek remedies:

I used to take a genuine interest in others, try to disentangle their problems and prevent threatened separations, so that they should not undergo what I had undergone. So they used to call me the confidant; also, because of my ramblings round the district, the wanderer. This—a balm to my spirits which I could find only in the open air, in valleys and on hills, in meadows and in forests—was something I owed to the position of Frankfurt, lying as it does between Darmstadt and Hamburg . . . . I acclimatized myself to living on the road, wandering back and forth like a courrier between mountain and plain . . . . As I went I would sing curious hymns and dithyrambs to myself, of which one has survived under the title of 'The Wanderer's Storm-Song.' I sang this sort of semi-nonsense verse passionately to myself when I ran into a fearful storm and had to make headway against it.

Here are a few lines out of this 'semi-nonsense':

> Whom thou desertest not, Genius,
> Nor the rain, nor the storm
> Sends breath of horror over his heart.
> Whom thou desertest not, Genius,

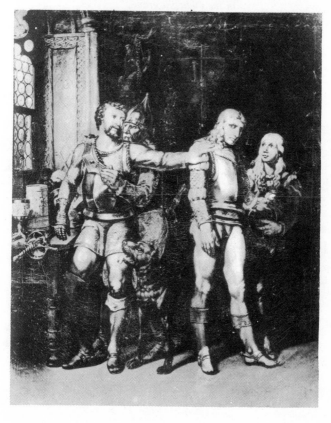

Goetz von Berlichingen with his prisoner Weislingen.
Painting by Tischbein, Zürich 1782.

Shall to the rain-cloud,
Shall to the hail-storm,
Sing his challenge,
Like the lark—
You, up there.

. . . Whom thou desertest not, Genius,
Downy wings shalt thou spread under him
When he sleeps upon the crag;
With guardian pinions shalt thou cover him
In the midnight grove . . .

This is *Sturm und Drang*, literally and figuratively. The swarthy little peasant whom he meets, the gods of Olympus, his own feelings and thoughts, the memory of Pindar, of Anacreon, of Theocritus, all mingle together in his song. The poet is here the very soul of the cosmos.

View of Wetzlar on the Lahn in the 18th century.

He was now what Herder and Friederike had made him—ore freed from its dross—and was to remain so: a Goethe with no more doubts about himself, and so henceforth the true Goethe. Shakespeare remained his great model—that 'Will of all Wills' upon whom he lavished some enthusiastic writing on the occasion of a celebration in his honor on the 14th of October 1771:

The first page of his that I read made me his for life, and when I had come to the end of the first play I stood there like a man born blind and given his sight, in a moment of time, by some wonder-working hand.

He flays all the people who have failed to understand him: the French, the Germans, Voltaire, even Wieland:

And my cry is, nature, nature! Nothing is so wholly nature as Shakespeare's men and women.... And what does our century think it understands about passing judgment upon nature? Whence are we to know her—we who, from our youth up, have had everything all tight-laced and trimmed up, both what we have felt in ourselves and what we have seen in others?

He was full of plans. Since his Strasbourg days he had been thinking of writing a play about Caesar. He confided to Herder that he had been studying the life and death of Socrates and 'putting them into dialogue in his head.' His ideas for *Faust* and *Goetz von Berlichingen* were well advanced. He wrote to Salzmann, on the 28th of November 1771:

You know me so well, and yet I will wager you cannot guess why I am not writing.... My whole mind is engaged in an enterprise which is making me forget Homer and Shakespeare and everything else. I am writing a play about the story of one of the noblest men of Germany; I am rescuing the memory of a valiant man...

The cold historical truth is that this 'valiant man,' Goetz von Berlichingen, was a robber-baron; but Goethe made him into a 'strong' personality embodying the *Sturm und Drang* ideal, a hero of liberty battling with the mediocrities of his day. Strasbourg Cathedral had aroused his enthusiasm for Germany's past. He plunged into a study of fifteenth- and sixteenth-century society, the background to his 'titan.' Hence he very willingly accepted an opportunity now offered him to go to Wetzlar, where he would have leisure to immerse himself in the past history of the Holy Roman Empire of the German Nation.

VIII. Wetzlar:
May to September 1772

Kestner, Lotte, Goethe: the genesis of Werther.

Wetzlar was, in fact, the center for the twenty-thousand-odd lawsuits then pending within the Holy Empire. Young lawyers used to go there to try their hand at disentangling these long-standing cases. Goethe had qualified on the 25th of May 1772. It was just a year since he had written *May Day* for Friederike.

Since leaving behind, first the family circle at Sesenheim, and now my group of friends at Frankfurt and Darmstadt, I had been left with an emptiness in my heart which I could not fill. So I was in that condition in which, no sooner does an inclination approach us, in whatever guise, than it steals right upon us unawares and nullifies all our good resolutions.

He wrote to Herder, about the 10th of July 1772:

Courage, hope, fear and tranquillity occupy my breast in succession.... Now that I know nothing of you, the Greeks are my sole study.

Werther, in turn, was to be portrayed reading Homer.

In the idle, dreamy state in which he was—because nothing in the present moment sufficed to satisfy him—he found what he lacked in the friendship of this girl, who, while her scheme of living took in her entire year, yet seemed to live only for the current moment. She liked having him for her companion; and he was soon unable to do without her presence, for she was his link with the everyday world; so they were soon inseparable companions at her work all over the estate—in field and meadow, vegetable garden and flower garden. When her fiancé's business would allow him, he would share in this as well; they had all three got into the habit—without meaning to, or knowing how it had happened—of being unable to do without each other.

The records show that Goethe's memories were very exact; and show also how freely the details of the novel are borrowed from the reality. In life as in the book, Lotte had a host of small brothers and sisters, to whom, as mistress of the house, she was an admirable substitute for their dead mother. The occasion of

Lotte Kestner, née Buff,
from a pastel by Schröder (1782).

DAS AL...BECHHAUS

her first meeting with Goethe *was* a country ball to which they went in the same carriage. She was even wearing the white dress with pink ribbons immortalized in the novel. Goethe-Werther was as passionate as Lotte's fiancé, Kestner-Albert, was coolly rational. The only important difference here between fiction and life was that Lotte never returned Goethe's feeling for her.

Kestner wrote in a letter of the 18th of November 1772:

This common attachment, as we got to know each other better, made a very solid tie of friendship between him and me.... But even though he had to renounce all hope where Lotte was concerned, and in fact did renounce it, he could not, for all his philosophy and his natural pride, command himself so thoroughly as to overcome all his inclination for her. And his qualities are such that he might well become a danger to a young girl, especially one with good feeling and good taste; but Lotte was so well able to control him, and knew so well how to behave with him, that he was never able to nourish any hope, and indeed was forced to admire her attitude in the matter...

Once again, the only remedy lay in flight; and this time it was as salutary for them as for himself. Kestner wrote in his diary for the 10th of September:

At noon Dr. Goethe dined with me in the garden. I did not know that it would be for the last time.... In the evening, Dr. Goethe came to the 'German House' [Lotte's father's house.] He, Lotte and I had an odd conversation on the condition of the afterlife, departure and return, etc. It was Lotte, not he, who began it. We agreed between us that whichever of us died first should, if he could, give the survivors an account of that other life. Goethe was very depressed, because he knew that he was going to leave next day.

The ambiguous use in this conversation of 'departure' and 'return' inspired the two notes he wrote, one that same day and the other at the moment of leaving—emotional, direct, non-'literary,' 'thou' alternating with 'you.' This same conversation was to re-echo passionately in the novel, under the same date of the 10th of September.

Goethe to Charlotte Buff, 10th of September 1772:

I do indeed hope to return, but God knows when. Lotte, what I felt in my heart while you were speaking, knowing that it was the last time I should see you. No, not the last time; but I am leaving tomorrow. He is gone. What spirit was it which inspired you to start that discussion. It gave me the chance to say everything I felt—oh! what mattered to me was this world below, and your hand which I was kissing for the last time. The room which I shall never enter again, and your dear father who was coming with me for the last time. Now I am alone and I can weep; I am leaving you happy, and I am not being put out of your hearts. And I shall see you again; but not tomorrow, and it feels like never. Say to those boys of mine 'He is gone.' I can't go on.

11th of September 1772:

I've packed, Lotte, and it is dawn; in a quarter of an hour I shall be gone. You can share the pictures I forgot amongst the children, and that will let me off writing, Lotte, when I have nothing to write. For you know everything; you know how happy I have been during this time; and I am going to the best and dearest of people, but why away from you? So it is, and it is my fate that today, and tomorrow, and the day after tomorrow, I am unable to add what I have so often added jokingly. Keep a glad heart always, dear Lotte, you are happier than a hundred others, but you are not indifferent, and, dear Lotte, I am happy to be able to read in your eyes that you believe that I shall never change. Farewell, a thousand times farewell.

Garbenheim, near Wetzlar; Werther's "Wahlheim."
Werther's first meeting with Lotte. Having arrived to escort her to the ball he finds her cutting bread and butter for her little brothers and sisters.
(Engraving by Chodowiecki).

IX. Frankfurt:
September 1772 to October 1775

The 'titans': Prometheus – Ganymede –
The Wandering Jew – Werther – The first
version of Faust – Lili Schönemann.

'I shall never change.' Did he, then, believe that this new love was to last for ever? He was indeed never to change in the sense that he would always so charge the passing moment with joy and suffering as to attach to it an eternity of weight. Faust had not yet reached the point of saying that no moment could ever hold him.

He went home on foot, along the valley of the Lahn as far as Coblenz, where he was to meet Merck at the house of some mutual friends, the Von la Roche family. Their daughter, Maximiliane, did not fail to make an impression on his heart. The Lotte of the novel was to have her deep black eyes.

From now until the time when he went to Weimar, Frankfurt was to remain his center of gravity. These three continuous years there, interrupted only by his journey along the Rhine valley in July and August 1774 and his visit to Switzerland in July and August 1775, are amongst the most productive of his life.

He embarked on a vast correspondence, in which for months Kestner and Lotte held the most prominent place. She sent him the pink ribbons she had worn at their first meeting. 'That same flower-color; but it seems to me to be more faded than it was in the carriage, which is quite natural.' He thought much about their union, but Lotte and Kestner had the tact to conceal the exact date of their marriage from him.

He worked without intermission: collaborating in the production of a literary review, the *Frankfurter gelehrte Anzeigen;* publishing the 'Pastor's Letter' as an attack on pharisaism and intolerance; writing about German art; planning a play about Mahomet, which resulted in the production of a few fine fragments; the whole period punctuated by the composition of dramatic trifles for carnival performance and, to his father's great satisfaction, the practice of his legal profession.

In its first version, *Goetz* burst the confines of dramatic art, and Herder disliked it. Goethe revised it in a few weeks. He overcame the distaste for appearing in print which Behrisch had given him, and published the play at his own and Merck's expense, resulting in a loss. He sent Salzmann a copy intended for the family at Sesenheim: 'It may be some consolation to poor Friederike to see the traitor being poisoned.'

He was striving at this time to affirm his own independence in relation to his environment:

The surest foundation for it was my productive talent. For several years it had not deserted me for a moment; the things of which I was aware during the day even used, often enough, to take regular shape at night in my dreams; and when I opened my eyes there would dawn upon me either some fantastic new whole or else some part of something already in being. Usually I would write everything down very early in the day; but in the evening too, or even late at night, when wine and company had stimulated my vital spirits, people could demand such things of me at will; it needed only an occasion with some little character to it, and I was all ready at once. As I reflected on this natural gift, and found that it was entirely my own, and could be neither furthered nor hindered by anything alien to me, I came to like the idea of basing my whole existence upon it.

It was now that he began to be dominated by the image of Prometheus, a being independent of the gods, and to consider the idea of making him the hero of a new play. This plan has bequeathed us a few passages of dialogue, and that great titanic ode in which *Sturm und Drang* found their most perfect expression. This poem, magnificent in its form, hurls at God a claim to independence which remains unique in Goethe's writing: let God remain within the bounds of his own realm; the earth is the domain of the creative artist.

> *Cover your heaven, Zeus,*
> *With a mist of cloud*
> *And busy yourself, like an urchin*
> *Slicing off thistle-heads,*
> *With oak-trees and with mountaintops;*
> *Yet this mine earth*
> *You must let stand as mine,*
> *And mine the cottage which you never built,*
> *And mine the hearth*
> *Whose glowing fire*
> *Is what you envy me.*

Nothing poorer do I know
Under the sun than you, o gods!
You wretchedly nourish
From a tribute of victims
And the breath of prayer
That majesty of yours,
And you'd starve, if it were not
That children and beggars
Are everhopeful fools.

When I was a child,
And knew not whence nor whither,
I turned my bewildered eyes
To the sun, as though there were up there
An ear to hear my lament,
A heart like mine
To take pity on one sore oppressed.

Who helped me
Against the Titans' arrogance?
Who saved me from death,
And from slavery?
Didst thou not bring all to good issue thyself,
O holy and glowing heart?
And then, all young and good, didst glow
Thine illusory thanks for salvation
To the Sleeper there on high?

I honor you? Wherefore?
Have you ever soothed the pangs
Of the heavy-laden?
Have you ever stilled the tears
Of the anguished?
Have I not been smithied into a man
By that omnipotent Time
And that eternal Fate
Which are my masters and yours?

Did you indeed suppose
That I should hate my life,
And flee into the waste
Because it is not all
Blossomy dreams that ripen?

> *Here do I sit, forming men*
> *To mine own image,*
> *A race that shall be like me,*
> *To suffer and to weep,*
> *To delight and to rejoice;*
> *And to have no care for you,*
> *Even as I!*

In his old age Goethe declared that this is to be interpreted only as a poetic theme—an attempt, perhaps, to tone down the effects of his youthful insolence.

About May 1773 he began to study Spinoza, 'whose mind was to have so great an influence on all my thought.' He admits elsewhere that he would be unable to state exactly how much of himself he read into the philosopher's writings. He seems to have interpreted him in a way consonant with the theosophical and mystical reading he had already done. It is not only that all things emanate from God and return to God—which would still imply a certain transcendence—but God and nature coalesce. The human soul aspires to communion with this God-Nature, an impersonal and immanent God. Shortly after *Prometheus* we have *Ganymede:* 'from one extreme to the other.'

> *In the sparkling morning*
> *How you glow around me,*
> *Spring, thou Beloved!*
> *With a thousand-fold ecstasy of love*
> *There strains at my heart*
> *A holy sense*
> *Of thine eternal blaze,*
> *Beauty without end!*
>
> *O that I might embrace you*
> *In this arm of mine!*
>
> *Ah, upon thy bosom*
> *Lying here, I languish,*
> *And thy blossoms, thy grass*
> *Thrust against my heart.*
> *Thou dost cool the burning*
> *Thirst of my bosom,*
> *Tender wind of morning!*
> *Within there calls the nightingale*
> *Tenderly to me from out the misty vale.*

The death of Werther.
(Engraving by Tony Johannot, 1844).

I come! I come!
Whither? O whither?
Up yonder! The thrust is upwards.
The clouds go floating
Upwards, those clouds
Are stooping to the yearning of love.
To me! To me!
Bearing me in you
Upwards!
Embracing embraced!
Upwards to thy bosom,
O all-loving Father!

He had drawn away from Pietism, because he could not believe in a radical corruption of human nature. He believed that there remained in it 'a certain seed' which can develop 'when brought to life by divine grace.... And since I could not be deprived of my attachment to the Holy Scriptures and to the Founder and the early confessors, I fashioned myself a Christianity for my own private use, and tried to give it foundations and a structure by assiduous study of history and close attention to those who had inclined to my mind in the matter.' Since with him everything must needs take a poetic form, these preoccupations suggested the idea of a play about the Wandering Jew.

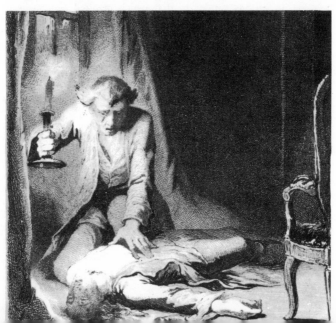

His mind was crowded with so many plans that he abandoned this as he did so many others. Despite his creative work and his moments of mystical exaltation he was still at times tormented by the thought of suicide. He toyed with it sometimes, laughed at himself, and tried, without success, to free himself from it completely by giving it literary form. It was then that he heard that his friend Jerusalem, secretary at a legation, had killed himself for love, 'and immediately after the general tidings of it reached me, came the most precise and circumstantial description of the event. That moment revealed the plan of *Werther;* the whole thing sped together and became a solid mass, as water in a vessel at the point of freezing can be turned into a block of ice by the slightest movement.'

His memories of that spring at Wetzlar (and perhaps of that other spring at Sesenheim, since he dated Werther's letters in that year, 1771), his meeting with Lotte and his love for her, his friendship with Kestner, with its sincerity tinged with jealousy, his religious transports in the bosom of nature, his fervor and his despair all found expression at once; so spontaneously that he needed only four weeks to write the novel, in the spring of 1774.

Werther

In the letter here quoted from the novel, Goethe has sought to express an ecstasy similar to that which inspired *Ganymede* by borrowing a Christian terminology suggestive of a personal God —the All-loving, All-powerful Being who created us in His own image—but we know that in all these expressions his true veneration is directed, confusedly, to the God-Nature of pantheism.

'10th May'

When the lovely valley is steaming all around me, and the sun, high in the sky, rests on the surface of the impenetrable darkness in my forest, where only a few isolated rays steal into the sanctuary within, and I lie in the deep grass by the tumbling brook, and the manifold thousands of little grasses growing closer to the soil begin to reveal their fascination; when I feel the humming of that little world between the grassblades, the countless, inexhaustible forms of tiny grubs and flies so close to my heart, and feel, too, the presence of the Almighty Being who created us to His own image, the breath of the All-loving Being who keeps and holds us floating in this endless bliss; oh my friend! then, when my eye dims, and the world all around me and the heaven above come to rest in my soul like the image of the beloved: then I am often seized with longing, and I think: Oh, if only you could give expression to this, if only you could breathe onto a sheet of paper all that lives so abundantly, so warmly within you, so that it would be the mirror of your soul as your soul is the mirror of the infinite God!—oh my friend!—but it defeats me, I am overwhelmed by the power of the splendor of these manifestations.

Nature, God-Nature, is good. But when unhappiness comes to Werther the problem of evil and suffering confronts him, ineluctably.

'18th August'

It is as though a curtain had been taken away from before my soul, and the theatre of endless life is changing before my eyes to the gulf of the ever-open grave. Is it possible to say 'This is,' since everything passes? Since everything rolls by as swift as thunder, so seldom even enduring to the full capacity of its being, alas, but swept away by the current, drowned and smashed against the rocks? There is never a moment in which you and yours are not decaying, never a moment in which you yourself are not, as you must *be, a destroyer; the most harmless of walks costs the lives of a thousand poor little grubs, and a single footstep is enough to shatter the ants' toilsome erections and to stamp a whole little world into a dishonored grave. Oh it is not the big, rare crises of the world— the floods which sweep your villages away, the earthquakes which swallow up your cities—which move me; what undermines my heart is this wasting power which lies hid in the totality of nature; which has formed nothing except what destroys its neighbor and itself. I am reeling under the stress of this anguish, with heaven and earth and all their interlocking forces around me: I can see nothing but a forever-devouring, forever-regurgitating monster.*

The Sorrows of Young Werther appeared in 1774. Its success was such as we, with the literary habits of the twentieth century, can scarcely imagine. Within a few weeks Goethe was famous throughout Europe, and soon afterwards among people of culture all over the Old and New Worlds, and even as far as China. There began to be a Werther style of dress among young men: the blue coat, yellow waistcoat and boots. It became impossible to keep count of all the criticisms, translations, imitations and parodies. As for Goethe himself:

I had the feeling which follows a general confession: I felt happy and free and ready for a new life. This time, the tried old remedy had stood me in wonderfully good stead. But while I felt lightened

*and clarified by having transmuted reality into poetry, it was a con-
fusion of mind in my friends to think that poetry ought to be transmuted into reality, and that one should imitate a novel of this sort
and actually shoot oneself; and this, which happened at the beginning
amongst only a few, began afterwards to occur in the public at large,
so that this little book, which had been so much help to me, got the
evil reputation of being highly pernicious.*

On his own testimony, he re-read *Werther* only once, and sedul-
ously refrained from revising it.

We should have to write in parallel columns in order to give a
chronological account of Goethe's activities during these years
between 1773 and 1775. 'He pulls manuscripts out of every corner
of his room,' said one of his visitors. And perhaps it would be
the best way of showing the many-sided aspects of him revealed
in his letters and writings.

Clavigo, a four-act tragedy founded on an incident told by
Beaumarchais, was written in a week at the beginning of 1774.
'Another traitor, a pendant to the Weislingen in *Goetz*,' he wrote,
thinking of Friederike.

Erwin und Elmire and *Claudine von Villa Bella* are plays with
music. There were satires and farces: *Gods, Heroes and Wieland*,
for example, and *The Marriage of Hanswurst*. *Stella* is a play
about a man torn between two loves, a situation in which Goethe
himself was several times to be. Meanwhile he prepared briefs
and made contributions to Lavater's 'Physiognomical Fragments.'
He also had an innumerable series of visitors, some of them from
considerable distances, who came to meet him as a famous author.

The First Version of Faust

The finest fruit of these restless years and their abundance of
work is the first version of *Faust*, the *Urfaust*, which was incorporated into Goethe's final version of the work. It was not
rediscovered in its original form until 1887. Goethe was cautious
in showing the manuscript, and only did so to a few select friends.

The famous adventurer and magician, one part history to three
of legend, who pledged his soul to the devil in exchange for
earthly pleasures, was the hero of a fifteenth-century book which
won immediate popularity. In the sixteenth century he inspired
Marlowe's tragedy. The tradition remained alive. In his childhod,
Johann Wolfgang may have seen his story enacted in the puppet
theatres at the Frankfurt fair.

The *Faust* of 1773-5 begins with the famous monologue in which the hero proclaims his disgust with all academic learning, as young Goethe had done at Leipzig:

> *Now, alas! of philosophy*
> *And medicine and law*
> *And, twice alas, of theology too,*
> *I've made thorough study, with fervent toil.*
> *Now here I stand, poor fool that I am,*
> *And still as wise as I was before.*

Goethe now recalls his alchemical books. Faust conjures the Spirit of the Earth in accents expressing all the extravagant titanism of Goethe's youth:

> *I have a mind to adventure in the world,*
> *To bear all woes of earth and all her joy,*
> *To battle at large with storms,*
> *And in the grind of shipwreck not to flinch.*

The Spirit of the Earth consents to reveal itself, and at first mocks at the terror with which its appearance overwhelms this mortal man:

SPIRIT: ... *What pitiful terror*
Seizes upon thee, Superhuman One!...
FAUST: ...*'Tis I, I am Faust, I am thine equal.*
SPIRIT: *In the floods of life, in the storm of doing*
I ebb and flow,
Weaving hither and thither,
Birth and grave,
An unending sea,
A changing weft,
A glowing life!
So I work at the murmuring loom of time
And fashion the Godhead's living robe.
FAUST: *Thou who dost wander the wide world's round,*
Laborious Spirit, how near I feel to thee.
SPIRIT: *Thou art the equal of that spirit whom thou canst hold,*
Not mine! [vanishes]
FAUST: *Not thine!*
Whose then?
I the image and likeness of the Godhead!
And not even thine!

Exaltation and despair alternate, going 'from one extreme to the other,' as in Werther.

In contrast with Faust's aspirations, his desire to penetrate the very mysteries of the cosmos, his *famulus* Wagner feels he would be content with what he thinks are more accessible truths: the heart and mind of man. Faust replies:

> *The few who have known something of them,*
> *Who, fool enough, barred not their brimming hearts*
> *But opened sense and vision to the mob*
> *Have from all time been crucified and burnt.*

Then comes the scene in which Mephistopheles hoaxes the student, giving him burlesque sketches of all the pedantic learning of the universities. Finally he recommends to him that ancient saying of 'my relative, the serpent': '*You shall be as gods, knowing good and evil.*'

Then comes Auerbach's wine-cellar—another memory of Leipzig: a comic interlude, for there was a Goethe who was not only a satirist but a comedian and even a downright clown. He is little discussed, perhaps because people seem to fear a diminution of the serious-minded, noble Goethe. The other one was capable of laughing for the pure pleasure of laughing, as witness the song about the king's favorite flea, or the Rat Song. It was Shakespeare, with his violent juxtapositions of farce and tragedy, who had shown the way here, too.

Side by side with the drama of the intellect runs the drama of the heart, where the images of Gretchen and Friederike coalesce. The *Urfaust* already includes the dialogue of the first meeting, the dispatch of the casket, the ballad of the King of Thule and the jewel scene, Frau Marthe's garden and Mephisto's witticisms, the seduction of Gretchen, and what neither Faust nor the devil had foreseen: his love for her, for Faust was no more capable than Goethe himself of seducing anyone without losing his entire heart to her.

Gretchen, pious and innocent, desires to know whether Faust believes in God. This provides Goethe with an occasion for a new profession of faith:

> *Who can name Him?*
> *And who confess:*
> *I believe in Him?*
> *Who, feeling aught,*

> *Can bring himself*
> *To say: I do not believe?*
> *The All-embracing,*
> *The All-sustaining,*
> *Does He not enfold*
> *You, and me, and Himself?*
> *Does not heaven arch above us there?*
> *Does not firm earth lie here below?*
> *And do there not, on every hand,*
> *Rise the eternal stars?*
> *Do my eyes not gaze into yours?*
> *And do not all things*
> *Throng upon your head and heart*
> *And weave in endless mystery*
> *A web invisible and visible about you?*
> *Fill your heart to its full depth with this,*
> *And then, when all the bliss of feeling it is yours,*
> *Call it what you will,*
> *Call it joy! heart! love! God!*
> *For me, I have no name*
> *For it. Feeling is all,*
> *A name is noise and smoke,*
> *Beclouding the fire of heaven.*

Is this God-Nature, or the God of Christianity? Gretchen, in her simplicity and purity of heart, at least grasps that Faust speaks with respect of God.

GRETCHEN: *All that is very fine and good;*
> *It is much the same as the catechism says,*
> *Only in slightly different words.*

FAUST: *It is said in all places*
> *By all hearts under the light of heaven,*
> *Each in his own speech,*
> *Why not by me in mine?*

Then come the conversation at the well, where Gretchen's friend speaks with scorn of girls who sin, the wonderful prayer she addresses in her desolation to Our Lady of Sorrows, the funeral of her mother, the curse of Valentin, and the prison scene: rather than flee with him who has dragged her into crime, Gretchen accepts death as expiation.

One of Goethe's friends wrote on the 17th of October 1774; 'Faust is nearly finished.' Goethe himself did not know that this work was to keep him company for another sixty years, until the very end of his life.

Lili Schönemann

At about the same time that he was writing this story, Goethe was enacting another; for he was incapable of remaining long out of love.

One evening a friend of his took him to a concert in the house of a rich Frankfurt businessman. The only daughter of the family played the harpsichord. He found her charming. They exchanged a few friendly words in the course of the evening and never took their eyes off each other during the remainder of the concert. Lili Schönemann—rich, spoiled, and at this time sixteen years old—told him shortly afterwards that she had wanted to prove the power of her charm upon him and had been punished for it,

Lili Schönemann,
as Baroness von
Türckheim (Pastel, 1782).

for she found she was caught herself. Naturally enough, this confession was enough to complete the conquest of the young man. There followed a necessity on both sides of seeing each other. 'I could not do without her nor she without me.' This meant that he was forced to go back again into Lili's fashionable world:

> Is this myself, whom you amid all these lights
> Hold at the card-table?
> And whom you often put confronting faces
> Which are so unendurable?
> The flowers of spring now hold no greater charm
> For me, on the meadow there;
> Angel, where you are, there is love and goodness,
> Where you are, nature is there.

To his pen-friend—whom he never met—Auguste zu Stolberg, a confidante whom he could trust, he wrote on the 13th of February 1775:

If, my dear friend, you can imagine a Goethe in a laced coat, and in gallantry to match from head to foot, in the midst of a meaningless splendor and brilliance of brackets and chandeliers, and with all kinds of people round him, held fast to a card-table by a pair of bright eyes; and then, for a change of distraction, led from reception to concert and from concert to ball, and courting a delicious golden-haired creature, with the utmost degree of frivolous attentiveness, then you have the fancydress Goethe of the moment, the man who lately stammered out some of his confused and deeply-felt ideas to you...

But there is another, the one in the grey beaver coat and the brown silk necktie, and boots, who can sense spring already in the sharp February air; for whom the wide world which he loves will soon be opening again, and who, forever active and striving and working within himself, tries in turn, in his own measure, to express the innocent feelings of youth in little poems, the strong spice of life in all kinds of plays, the silhouettes of his friends, his landscape and his beloved home in charcoal on grey paper; and who makes no enquiries to right or left about how people judge what he does, because he is always working his way up one step further, and does not want to jump at any ideal but only to let his feelings develop into capabilities while he goes on battling and playing.

So he was feeling the summons of Nature. With a few friends, including the two Counts zu Stolberg, Auguste's brothers, he

planned a visit to Switzerland. They left Frankfurt on the 14th
of May. In the course of the journey they met the Duke of Saxe-
Weimar, Lavater, and other admirers of Goethe. But even the
beauty of the scenery was unable to distract him from his love,
and on the lake of Zürich his thoughts were full of Lili:

> Eyes, my eyes, O why sink down?
> Golden dreams, do you come again?
> Away, o dream! Though thou be gold
> Here are love and life also.
>
> On the wave are flashing
> A thousand wavering stars,
> Softly clouds are washing
> The towery hills afar;
> The wind of morning flurries
> Round inlets deep in shade
> And in the water's mirror
> The ripening fruit's displayed.

The journey did him good; yet he was so dissatisfied with
himself, despite the teeming productivity of the last few years,
that he wrote in a letter of the 17th of August 1775: 'I have written
all kinds of things, relatively little, and, at bottom, nothing.'

Once back in Frankfurt, he began playing his part once more
as one of the 'menagerie' of the flirtatious Lili's admirers. He had
to make an end. Moreover, the two families were both, for
different reasons, unwilling to approve the marriage. 'What you
say about Lili is entirely true,' he wrote. 'But alas, what divides
me from her only makes the magic bond which unites me to her
stronger than ever.' And a few days later: 'I have had a terrible
week, from every point of view, but I have held out.' (September
1775.)

Once more, the remedy was to be flight. He was given an
opportunity: the Duke and Duchess of Weimar had invited him
to court. A new carriage was to be sent for him about the 13th
of October. He said good-bye to everyone. But the carriage did
not come. Counsellor Goethe tried to convince his son that his
aristocratic friends had been making game of him. Locked in his
room, Goethe worked away at *Egmont*, his new play. Its heroine,
Klärchen, sings the song of his own soul:

> Joyful
> And woeful,
> And thoughtful to be,

> *Longing*
> *And fearing*
> *In wavering distress,*
> *For joy, shouting sky-high,*
> *For sorrow, near death,*
> *Happy is none*
> *But the soul that's in love.*

The days went by. After nightfall, it would become unbearable. Wrapped in a heavy cloak, he used to go and stand by Lili's windows. One evening he heard her singing, and accompanying herself on the harpsichord; the song was one he had written for her barely a year before, '*Why Draw me Irresistibly...*' So as to hear better, he laid his ear against the projecting lattice of the window. He tried, unsuccessfully, to catch a glimpse of her lovely form through the thick curtains. He was kept from going in only by his firm determination to avoid giving her pain by his presence, and to make his renunciation of her real.

An existence of this sort, practically in hiding, could not go on indefinitely. He decided to fall in with his father's plan and go away to Italy. We have his impressions of the parting in the beginning of a travel-diary, written at Ebersstadt where he had made a halt at midday:

30th of October 1775... *In the corn-market, Spengler's boy was putting up his stall with a great clatter, and bowing to the neighbors' maid-servant in the depressing rain. That bow was a sort of omen of the events of the day. Ah! I thought, who then.... No, I said, there was indeed a time.... He who has memories should be envious of none.... Farewell, Lili, farewell for the second time! The first time, I went away full of hope that our destinies might be united. Now it is decided that we are to play our parts separately. At this moment, I have no fear either for you or for myself, confused though things seem to be. Farewell. AND YOU, what shall I call you, you whom I bear on my heart like a spring flower? You shall be called 'exquisite flower.' How shall I say farewell to you? Be of good heart, it is not too late.... It was high time indeed.... Another few days, and then.... Oh farewell! Am I in this world for nothing but to struggle thus, eternally guilty and not-guilty?'*

Who was this unknown? She, perhaps, whom he met at Offenbach, and of whom he wrote to Auguste zu Stolberg: 'I am going to a dance, for love of a sweet creature.' His multitudinous heart suffered from many loves at once, and suffered too from being a cause of suffering.

He had got no further than Heidelberg, where he was staying with an old family friend, Fräulein Delph, when a messenger came hurrying after him. It was simply that the ducal carriage had been delayed. Without hesitation, he obeyed the call of fate symbolized by the postillion's horn sounding through the night, and left once more for the north.

After her marriage, Lili became a very different woman from what might have been expected from her frivolous youth. She became the Baroness von Türckheim, and was living in Alsace at the outbreak of the Revolution. In 1792 she was offered a refuge at Heidelberg by that same Fräulein Delph who had been Goethe's hostess in 1775, but she refused, wishing to share whatever should befall her husband. He was eventually forced to cross the frontier, and she rejoined him disguised as a peasant, bringing with her their five children and carrying the youngest on her back.

Comparisons between Goethe's love-affairs are difficult. Friederike was the only one for whom he felt 'guilty and not-guilty.' Over the others he felt suffering and regret, but not remorse. Lili had been dead thirteen years when he said to Soret on the 5th of March 1830:

I was never so near to happiness [i.e., as at the period of his love for Lili]; *nor did any insuperable obstacle stand in the way of our union, and yet I could not marry her.*

She was the first whom I deeply and genuinely loved; and perhaps she was the last: for none of the affections of that sort to which I surrendered later went very deep in comparison with that one ...

The first! Gretchen—Annette—Friederike—Lotte! The last! And what of Frau von Stein, whose reign lasted for ten years, and Christiane Vulpius, who became his wife, and Ulrike, his last passion? (to mention only the 'princesses' and ignore the 'nymphs,' in Heine's words)? We must remember that when he made this confession to Soret he had just seen a lovely young girl who was a near relative of the Baroness von Türckheim, and the beloved image had risen so vividly from the past that it had made him, at least for the moment, forget all the others.

But in any case, at the point which we have now reached he was only twenty-seven years old. The fine new carriage was bearing him across Thuringia on the road to Weimar. He was going for a visit of a few months. He was to remain there the rest of his life.

X. The First Ten Years at Weimar:
   1776 to 1786

> *Goethe as a ducal administrator – Frau*
> *von Stein – Iphigenie – Review of past*
> *years – 'Wanderer's Night Song' – 'The*
> *pyramid of my existence...' – Tasso –*
> Egmont – *The 'Hymn to Nature' – The*
> *inter-maxillary bone – Weariness – Flight.*

The miniature Duchy of Saxe-Weimar, whose capital counted a population of about eight thousand, had, until the eve of the events we are describing, the Duchess Anna Amalia for its moving spirit. She was a niece of Frederick II, married in 1756 at the age of sixteen to the Duke of Weimar, and widowed in 1758. She handled the affairs of the state competently during the difficult period of the Seven Years' War. A woman of altogether exceptional intelligence and culture, she had made it her care to give her two sons a virile education, and when their childhood was over she chose no less a tutor for them than Wieland.

On the 3rd of September 1775, his eighteenth birthday, Duke Karl August assumed the supreme power. On the 3rd of October he married Princess Louise of Hesse-Darmstadt, the same age as himself. His was an energetic, violent, 'demonic' character, contrasting with the retiring nature of his young brother Konstantin and with his gentle, timid wife. She was later to suffer from her husband's character and his infidelities, and to withdraw into a resigned semi-retirement.

At the time when Goethe arrived, the Duke was revelling in his independence. In order to win an ascendancy over him, his new mentor was obliged to fling himself into his extravagant occupations—riding round the countryside, taking part in noisy revels by day and night, joining in village dances, and making love to girls in inns. He was in no way averse to lending himself to all this: 'My life goes by like a sleigh-ride, here and there, at top speed, bells jingling: God knows to what destiny such an education is to lead.' (22nd November 1775.)

Duke Karl August. (Pastel by Schröder, 1784).

This fooling went on for three months. After that, Goethe remained 'master of the revels' only in connection with the quieter distractions of masques and court functions. What was to matter henceforward was administration and, of course, love.

I shall certainly stay, and play my part as well as I can for as long as fate and I shall please.... Here at least I have a few duke-doms before me. I am at the moment only becoming acquainted with the country, and already I find it very pleasing. And the Duke is thus developing a taste for work... [14th February 1776.] *I have tried court life, and now I am going to try government...* [8th March].

The powers already in possession began by protesting against the intrusion of a man whose only testimonial was a famous novel.

But his charm soon began to affect them. Whether in sincerity or policy, Wieland was the first to succumb. Prince Konstantin's tutor, Knebel, was always to remain a faithful friend. The feminine element, including the two duchesses and their ladies-in-waiting, did not long hold out.

As an inducement to the poet to stay with him, Karl August gave him a house and garden at the edge of the town, and sent for Herder to be religious superintendant of the Duchy. When he gave Goethe a place on his Council, in June 1776, he had difficulty in persuading his chief minister, Von Fritsch, the leader of the malcontents, to withdraw his resignation. But Goethe succeeded in conciliating even him. He was thus firmly established at Weimar.

> *Over there upon the bank are standing*
> *Friends and dear ones, trembling on the dry ground:*
> *Oh, alas, why did he not remain here!*
> *Alas, the storm! Off course, and out of luck!...*
>
> *Yet at the tiller manfully he stands:*
> *The plaything of the wind and waves his ship,*
> *Of wind and waves no plaything is his heart.*
> *His mastering eye turned on the grim abyss,*
> *His trust is given, in shipwreck or in landfall,*
> *Unto his gods.*

Wieland, by Graff.

The house by the Ilm.

The 'government' of the duchy could be given the more modest name of administration. Goethe took his work seriously, content to enrich his personality with human contacts and new acquaintances. He devoted himself to renovating the mines at Ilmenau, and discussed the finances of the duchy, its police and its legislation, with the Duke. He was sometimes glad to be working like this: 'The weight of affairs is very beneficial to the soul; when it lays down the burden, it feels all the freer to play and rejoice in life.' At other times he was conscious of his difficulties: 'No one knows what I am doing, nor how many enemies I have to struggle against to achieve the least thing.'

In January 1779 he was given the administration of the army, and strove to cut the cost of it. He was president of the commission for architecture, and supervised the maintenance of roads; during these first ten years at Weimar he gradually became a sort of factotum for the duchy. In 1782 he was promoted to the rank of first minister, and given a patent of nobility to avoid any shock to the good old aristocratic tradition.

He began more and more to see his task as service of the community. He carried through a regulation for the prevention of fire, turned his attention to the condition of the cloth-workers of Apolda whose trade was inadequate to provide them with subsistence, and tried, so as to keep taxes down, to dissuade the Duke from his alliance with Prussia, which would lead to war, and to interest him in the good of his subjects. 'That prince, who is my whole happiness and my whole care...' He tried too to moderate his passion for hunting, which could be indulged only at the cost of greater misery for charcoalburners and peasants.

> *He who strives to lead others well*
> *Must be capable of denying himself much.*

These lines are from the poem which he dedicated to the Duke on his twenty-sixth birthday. Nothing could be further removed from the attitude of a courtier.

Frau von Stein

Nevertheless, the central focus of his thought throughout these first years at Weimar bore the name of Charlotte von Stein. She was born in 1742, the daughter of one Von Schardt, a marshal of the court, and of a Scottish woman of noble birth. So she was seven years older than Goethe. She had been a lady of the court since 1758, and had in 1764 married Freiherr von Stein, the Duke's Master of the Horse, a decent enough man, somewhat dour in manner, with no gifts beyond competence for his post. She had had seven children in ten years, of whom three boys remained alive. She was small, slight, dark-haired, with great black eyes; graceful and elegant, with a walk 'like a passing zephyr.' Of a melancholy, gentle, sickly disposition, she spent most of her time in retirement in her house at Kochberg. Goethe met her for the first time in December 1775. His earliest note to her is dated January 1776. We have about seventeen hundred of his letters to her, love-letters written in joy and in sorrow, often hastily scribbled and always wholly spontaneous and simple in their expression. But we have only this one side of the dialogue between them, for the letters she wrote to him were destroyed.

Once more tumult was breaking out in his heart.

Dear angel, I sent for my letters and was distressed that there was no word from you—not so much as a pencilled word, not a good-night. Dearest lady, be content that I should love you so much. If I can love anyone else still more I shall tell you. I shall leave you in peace.... You do not understand how dear you are to me. (28th of January 1776.)

Even in this first January he was already calling her *Besänftigerin*, giver of gentle peace. But we should not anticipate. The first of the 'Wanderer's Night-songs' expresses no more than a yearning after peace, not a peace already achieved. It was written on the 12th of February 1776:

> *Thou who art from heaven,*
> *Every grief and pain dost still,*
> *Him who is doubly wretched*
> *Doubly with fresh life dost fill—*
> *Ah, I'm weary of being driven!*
> *What's all the pain and pleasure for?*
> *Sweet peace,*
> *Come, oh come into my breast!*

That March, Frau von Stein told her doctor that Goethe had addressed her with the familiar 'du,' and that she had rebuked him. He had got up, strode about the room looking for his stick, failed to find it, and left without a word. 'I feel that Goethe and I are never going to be friends.' During that same month he went to Leipzig, saw Annette, now married, and was captivated, quite unplatonically, by the beautiful actress Corona Schröter: 'If only God would give me a woman like her, so that I could leave you in peace,' he wrote to Charlotte von Stein. 'But she is not sufficiently like you...'

He wrote to Wieland in April: 'I cannot explain the importance and power which this woman has for me except in terms of metempsychosis. Yes; we were once husband and wife. What we know of one another is now veiled in a spiritual cloud. I have no name for what we are: the past... the future... the Whole...'

The poem which he sent to Charlotte on the 14th of April, one of the pinnacles of his art, develops the same theme. Other hearts in love seek each other and never find each other:

> *To us two alone, poor loving beings,*
> *Is that mutual happiness denied*
> *Of living without ever understanding,*

78

Of seeing each other as we never were,
Of going forth afresh to each false joy-dream
And faltering, too, at every dream of fear . . .

Tell me, what is fate preparing for us?
Tell, how could it bind so sheer and tight?
Ah, in ages we have lived already
Thou my sister wast, or else my wife.

Thou didst know each trait within my being,
Discern the note of every separate nerve,
Thou couldst with a single glance then scan me,
Whom a mortal eye can hardly pierce;
Tempering drops on this hot blood thou sheddest,
Didst correct my wild and wandering course,
And, through resting in thine angel-arms,
This shattered heart would rouse itself once more . . .

And of all this still there floats a memory,
Only that, round our uncertain hearts,
Which feel that former truth unchanged within them,
And find the pain of this new state is hard.
To us it seems we have but half our souls,
For us it's twilight on the brightest day.
Joy it is that fate, which thus torments us,
Yet cannot make us change.

'Farewell, dear sister, since it must be so.' (16th of April 1776.)
'My love for you is a perpetual resignation . . .' (2nd of May.) At
least, let her not deprive him of her presence, which alone can
give him 'peace and strength. . . . And this only because of other
people.' Her 'presence' is a perpetually recurring theme. The
calm joy of that former life is something which he is far from
being able to taste, unchanged, in this one: 'Why must I torment
you! Dearest creature! We can be nothing to each other, and
we are too much to each other . . . But it is just because I see
things simply as they are that it drives me mad. . . . Anything I
could say would be stupid. In future I will look at you as we look
at the stars.' (June 1776.)

When she left Weimar for Kochberg and would not allow him
to join her there, he compared her to a madonna going up to
heaven, indifferent to those who remain behind. She replied on

the back of this note: 'Whether what I feel is evil or not, and whether I must expiate this sin which is so dear to me, my conscience does not tell me. Blot it out, O heaven, if ever it is to accuse me.' 'Alas, these eight weeks have choked up much that was in me,' he wrote to her on the 8th of November. 'I am still the same sensual person.' This was the time when Corona Schröter had been engaged to act in the court theatre at Weimar, and he was rehearsing *Die Mitschuldigen* with her.

Throughout these years he was on the search for himself. His 'two souls' were fighting within him: he was still Werther, now in love with another Charlotte, the Goethe of *Sturm und Drang*,

The lovely actress and singer Corona Schröter who, at Goethe's suggestion, was summoned to the court at Weimar in 1776. She created a passing rivalry between Karl August and Goethe.

the wanderer. In the middle of the frozen winter of 1777 he went alone, on horseback through the Harz, to see a young man with whom he had been corresponding, and whom he saw as the precise image of his own former soul; he climbed in December to the summit of the Brocken. 'When I am alone like this, I really recognize myself, just as I was in my early youth.' *Harzreise im Winter* is a sequel to the 'Wanderer's Storm Song':

> *But swathe the lonely soul*
> *In thy golden clouds!*
> *Encircle with winter's greenery,*
> *Till the rose grows full again,*
> *The rain-wet hair,*
> *O Love, of thy poet!*
>
> *With dim-flickering torch*
> *Thou dost light him*
> *Across the fords at night,*
> *Over foundationless roads*
> *On desolate open lands...*

And then there was the other Goethe beginning to take shape within him: the man who was becoming master of himself, and, in consequence, was already practicing renunciation and adapting himself to society—to the world, in every sense of the word. 'That is allowed which is pleasing,' says Tasso to the Princess, in the play which he was now beginning to plan. 'That is allowed which is seemly,' she replies. Frau von Stein's tempering of his natural impetuosity was going far beyond surface expression; it reached his heart and his very genius, presenting him with the image of 'measure,' nobility and harmony: the 'Greek' ideal of humanity.

At about the end of 1777 the letters take on a calmer tone. 'It seems that a change is taking place within me, but I do not yet know how to interpret it' (11th of February 1778). He sends books to his beloved, and flowers and fruit from his garden, to which he is devoting enthusiastic attention. He takes an interest in her house and children, especially five-year-old Fritz, with whom he has become great friends. She is still his gentle confidante, and as dear to him as ever: 'If I return to earth again, I will ask the gods to let me love only once; and if you were such an enemy to this world, I would ask that you should be that dear traveling companion' (2nd of March 1779).

Though she appears in his diary under the emblem of the sun, her influence on him was rather that of the gentle radiance of that night of which he wrote

>...*Dost the dear vale fill once more*
>*Stilly with cloudy sheen,*
>*And at last and once for all*
>*My soul dost wholly free;*
>
>*Spreadest over all my land*
>*Soothingly thy gaze,*
>*As my dearest's mild eye*
>*Does upon my fate.*

Iphigenie auf Tauris

Besides the poems he was writing, he intended to give symbolic expression in dramatic form to his search for the interior balance which Charlotte von Stein was to give him and was giving him already. The first, prose, version of *Iphigenie* dates from the beginning of 1779 (Act IV was written in one day!). He revised it in 1780 and went back to it again in Italy; it appeared in 1787 in its final verse form, with little alteration in its basic structure.

He follows Euripides in showing us Iphigenia as having been transported to Tauris, where she has become the priestess of her savior, Diana. She desires, by her own upright life, 'with pure hand and pure heart,' to wipe out the curse which weighs upon her race. By her gentleness, she has won from the Scythian King the suppression of human sacrifice; but in his disappointment at her refusal to marry him he is thinking of re-establishing it. As it happens, two strangers have just landed on the coast. Orestes, who has murdered his mother and is being pursued by the Furies, has been promised by the oracle that he will be delivered from them if he brings back 'the sister.' Pylades and he think that the oracle means Diana, sister of Apollo. Iphigenia, revealing herself, speaks words of peace:

ORESTES: *Then is this fire to be forever enkindled and nourished with hell's sulphur to burn upon my soul?*
IPHIGENIA: *Sweet incense do I bring to it. O let the breath of love touch thy breast—not unwelcome...*

After a final crisis, Orestes, under Iphigenia's influence, recovers his spiritual balance:

> *Methinks I hear far off the thunderous sound of the fleeing chorus of the Furies closing the door of Tartarus behind them...*
>
> *...It was by thy touch that I was to be wondrously healed. In thine arms that evil, sent from the gods, fastened all its claws in me once more, horribly wringing, for the last time, my very marrow, and then fled away like a snake to its hole; and now, through thee, I enjoy the light of day.*

When, that same year, 1779, Goethe was making preparations for accompanying the Duke to Switzerland in September, and wrote to let his mother know that he hoped to stay in the old house in the Deers' Ditch in Frankfurt, his letter reads like a self-compensation for the bitterness of earlier days. He is no longer a 'castaway':

> *I have everything a human being can desire, a life in which I can exert myself and grow day by day; I am coming, this time, in good health, without passion, without confusion, without trouble or agitation, but like one beloved of God who has completed one half of his existence, who, because of his past sufferings, can allow himself to hope for good things in future, and whose heart has also been tried in preparation for future sufferings.* (9th of August 1779.)

But two days earlier, face to face with himself in solitude, on the eve of his thirtieth birthday, the examination of conscience he made in his diary has a quite different ring:

> *Stayed at home, looked over my papers, burned old ones. Past interests of past days. Silent review of my life, its confusion and agitation and the desire for knowledge in which youth wanders in all directions looking for something satisfying. How I have delighted above all in mysteries, in obscure imaginary relationships. How I have made only a half-hearted attack on scientific knowledge, soon abandoned. How a sort of humble self-complacency runs through everything I was writing at that time. How shortsightedly I have moved amongst things human and divine. How little I have done, or even thought or written, usefully; how much time I have lost on feelings and shadows of passion, wasting days on them; how little value this has been to me; and now that half my life is gone, I have not made progress along the road; on the contrary, here I am like a man escaped from the water, just beginning to dry in the rays of the kindly sun. As for the time I have spent in worldly activity since October 1775, I dare not yet include it in my survey. May God continue to help us and grant us light, so that we may not get so*

much in our own way; may He grant us to do what is to be done from morning to evening, and give us a clear sense of the consequences of things...'

> *Upon every hill-top*
> *Is rest,*
> *In every tree-top*
> *Thou feelest*
> *Scarcely a breath;*
> *The small birds are quiet in the wood.*
> *Only wait, soon*
> *Thou too shalt rest.*

The untranslatable harmony of these lines, written in September 1780 on the inner wall of a wooden hunting-lodge on the Gickelhahn, near Ilmenau, could have been uttered only by a heart already at peace—one, perhaps, thinking of a yet more final peace.

1780-2 is the zenith of these ten years.

In March 1780 he thought of a new subject for a play, *Tasso:* it was doubtless intended from the first to glorify his beloved.

There was a new vigor in his assertion of his own personality and the part he had to play.

The daily task with which I am entrusted, which grows lighter and heavier every day, demands my presence, waking or dreaming—it is a duty which grows dearer to me every day; in this alone, and in nothing greater, do I desire to equal the greatest of men. This desire to build the pyramid of my existence as high into the air as possible —its base being given and established for me already—exceeds all else, and allows me scarcely a moment of forgetfulness. I must not delay, I am already advanced in years, perhaps fate will break me off in the middle, and this tower of Babel will remain truncated and incomplete. At least it shall be said that it was boldly conceived; and, if I live, my strength shall rear it on high, if God wills. (To Lavater, 20th of September 1780.)

In October 1780 there was a crisis in his relationship with Frau von Stein. He reproaches himself with having let her attitude draw words from him which hurt her:

Yes, it is a madness against one's own flesh when a wretch tries to relieve his feelings by hurting what he loves most.... It seems frightful to me to have ruined some of the best hours of our lives, those moments when we are together, when I would be willing to pull out the hairs of my head, one by one, if I could turn them into

85

anything that would please you—and then to be so blind and obstinate. Have pity on me. All this has become part of my state of mind, like a pandemonium full of invisible spirits; yet to a spectator, despite the fear he would feel if he were in it, it would seem only an infinitely empty vault. (10th of October 1780.)

It could well be Werther or Tasso speaking.

I thank you for your sympathy, my dearest. What can't be avoided must be borne. I only ask you to tell yourself every day that everything in me which may be displeasing to you comes from a source of which I am not master. (24th of November.)

It was between the 14th of October and the 14th of November that he wrote the first Act of *Tasso*, began the second, and then stopped.

On the long journey yesterday I thought about our story; it is strange enough. I compared my heart to a robber's castle, of which you have now taken possession; the evil rabble has been driven out, but you should consider, too, that it deserves a garrison: property is held only by jealous possession.... Go on with your good work, and let all the ties of love, friendship, necessity, passion and habit bind me faster to you every day... (8th of March 1781).

My soul has grown firmly into yours; I cannot enlarge upon this in words, you know that I cannot separate myself from you and that nothing from above or below can disunite us. I would that there were some vow or sacrament that might make me yours visibly and legally; how precious it would be to me! And my novitiate has indeed been long enough for reflexion. Farewell. I cannot write to you as 'Sie' any more, just as for a long while I could not speak to you as 'Du.' One word more on my devotions while traveling. The Jews have cords which they wind about their arms during the time of prayer; in the same way I wind your dear ribbon round my arm while I am praying to you, and so hoping for a share in your goodness, wisdom, moderation and patience. (12th of March 1781.)

After his return, there follow a few more notes; then, suddenly, at the end of March, the canticle of joy is sounding again:

My love is like the morning and the evening star... We have never lived such a lovely spring together before, may it never have an autumn!... I cannot tell you, nor is it given to me to understand what a transformation your love has wrought in me. This is a state which, despite my age, I have not known till now. Who ever learns all there is to learn of love?... Farewell, my New One.... May this openness and peace which you have given back to me be for you alone, and may all the good which results from it, both for others

86

The ducal park and the bridge over the Ilm in winter. The figures on the right are Goethe and little Fritz von Stein. On the left is Goethe's house. He probably made this drawing in the winter of 1778-9.

Frau von Stein, self-portrait.

*and for myself, be yours too. Believe me, I feel entirely different;
my former well-doing has returned, and with it my joy in life; you
have given me back my pleasure in doing good, which I had completely lost. I did it instinctively, and did not feel at ease.* (22nd
to 27th of March 1781.)

*Yesterday evening I had a great desire to fling my ring into the
water, like Polycrates, for in the quiet night I was reckoning up my
happiness and found it a colossal sum. Farewell, dearest, fulfilment
of my many thousand desires.* (22nd of April.) *Share in my peace
and happiness, since you have suffered so much with me, and know
how happy I am in your love.* (27th of April.)

In the course of that year he dedicated the following two poems
'to Lida' (written on the 20th and 22nd of September 1781):

I pity you, o you unhappy stars,
You who are beautiful and shine so glorious,
And on the hard-pressed sailor gladly twinkle,
Unrewarded both of gods and men:
For you love not, never love have known!
Unremitting do the eternal hours
Drive your courses through the width of heaven.
What a journey have you achieved already!
Since I, lingering in my dearest's arms,
Have of you and midnight been forgetful!

A goblet, finely-carved and full, I held,
Held it pressing it in both my hands,
Eager from its rim sweet wine was sucking,
Grief and care to drown there once for all.

In walked Amor, found me sitting there,
Deprecatingly he smiled on me,
As pitying me for lack of understanding.
'Friend, I know a vessel of greater beauty,
Worthy of sinking one's whole soul within it;
How will you reward me, if I grant it,
Fill it with another nectar for you?'

In what friendly fashion he kept his word!
Giving thee to me with soft affection,
Lida, after I for long had yearned.

When, embracing thy beloved body,
From these lips of thine, uniquely true,
I taste the balm of love for long conserved,
Blissful then unto my soul I say:

No, except for Amor, there's no god
Who ever such a vessel formed or owned!

After this, we will leave to their obstinacy that school of critics who maintain that even after this date their relationship was simply a 'marriage of souls.'

Tasso

It was, then, in a state of happiness that Goethe resumed his work in 1781. 'Don't you see what good care love takes of your poet? A few months ago, the next scene was impossible to write. Now, how easily it will pour out of my heart!' (25th of March 1781).

There is an echo of this in what he said to Eckermann in 1827:

I had Tasso's life, I had my own life, and as I mingled these two strange characters and their individualities the image of Tasso was born in me; in opposition to him I set Antonio, as a prosaic contrast, for whom there was again no lack of models. As for the other conditions of the court, of life, and of love, they were the same at Weimar as at Ferrara, and I can truly say of this creation that it is bone of my bone and flesh of my flesh.

For Weimar and Ferrara:

> *Around thy brother and thyself there gather*
> *Such minds and hearts as of you both are worthy...*
> *No name which Italy can name as great*
> *But has been named a guest within this house.*

For his friendship and misunderstandings with the Duke:

> *Man is not born for freedom, and there is*
> *To any noble soul, no fairer fortune*
> *Than this, to serve a prince he holds in honor.*
> *And so he is my lord, and I can feel*
> *The fullness of the scope of that great word.*
> *I now must learn to be silent when he speaks,*
> *And act when he commands it, even though*
> *Reason and heart may contradict with vigor.*

Thus spoke Frau von Stein, and thus speaks the Princess:

> *If thou wouldst learn aright of what is seemly,*
> *Then make enquiry only of noble women...*
> *Man strives for freedom, woman for moral good.*

And again it is Goethe-Tasso who answers:

> *O teach thou me to do what can be done!*
> *To thee are consecrated all my days.*
> *And when in praise of thee and thanks to thee*
> *My heart unfolds, then only do I feel*

The purest joy that can be felt by man,
The most divine in thee alone I know...
Whatever echo sounds in all my song
To one, *to one alone I owe it all!*
No vague and phantom form it is that hovers
Before my brow, now drawing near my soul
In dazzling splendor, now withdrawn again.
With these mine eyes I have seen the archetype
Of every virtue and of every beauty;
And what on this I've modeled will endure.

Goethe to Charlotte, April 1781: 'I have just been working at *Tasso*, and thus adoring you.... What I have written is certainly good, because it is an invocation addressed to you.'

TASSO: *I dreamt that I drew near the highest joy,*
And now this *joy is higher than any dream...*
What have I ever done, that she should choose me?
What shall I do, worthy of her to be?...
Hers am I, forming me she shall possess me,
My heart was keeping all its hoard for her...
      ... No, henceforth no more
Shall Tasso go alone 'midst trees,' midst men,
Losing himself, feeble and melancholy!
He is alone no more, he is with thee.

It is not surprising that he was now finding it difficult to finish *Egmont*, which had been on the stocks since Lili's day. How was he to harmonize, within one character, the hero of liberty and the careless nobleman, living by the impulse of the moment, a delmonic' type, hurrying, with eyes closed, to meet his fate? 'It is a strange play. If I had to write it again I should do it differently, and perhaps not at all' (20th of March 1782). Perhaps, too, Klärchen, Egmont's love, was too like Gretchen and Annette and the various girls of low station who had been in his life here and there, and not sufficiently like Frau von Stein.

The wisdom which the Princess teaches Tasso is to moderate himself, to accept order, to submit to measure. There is the same doctrine in *Grenzen der Menschheit*, 'Humanity's limits,' a poem which stands at the opposite pole to *Prometheus*.

When the arch-ancient
And holy Father
With calm hand serene
Out of rolling clouds
Blessing of lightnings
Sows upon the earth,
I kiss the ultimate
Hem of his garment,
Childlike awe stirs
Loyal in my heart.

For with gods
Shall not be measured
Any man whatever.
If he lifts himself upwards
So as to touch
His skull to the stars,
Then nowhere the soles
Of his unsure feet take hold,
And with him sport
The clouds and the winds...

What differentiates
Gods from men?
That many waves
Pass on before them
An ever-flowing stream:
Us the wave lifts,
Us the wave swallows,
And we go under.

Small is the ring
That bounds our life...

This search for interior balance and 'Greek' harmony meant that Goethe was now far removed from the mystical crises of his early youth. He was never to cease to believe in powers higher than man, but he called them indifferently God, the gods and fate. The name of Christ scarcely appears in his works again. He wrote to Lavater on the 29th of July 1782 that he was 'not an anti-Christian, not un-Christian, but decidedly a non-Christian.'

The religion to which he was turning was the humanitarian deism of Lessing and Herder and Freemasonry. In 1780 he was admitted to the Weimar Lodge, though he never became a very zealous initiate, and in 1783 he became one of the Gotha Illuminati. In 1784 he conceived the idea of a great poem which was to be once more an invocation to his beloved and at the same time was to teach wisdom to men. One of the two fragments of it became the dedication of his collected poems, the other appeared under the title of 'The Mysteries.' It is possible to discern here the traces of his alchemical studies in 1768-70, and also of more recent ones, particularly of the philosopher Saint-Martin. He depicts a Rosicrucian monastery, a sort of Montsarrat where the young man Markus is to be initiated. The old man who is the master of it, Humanus, has pronounced the rule:

> *From that power which every creature binds*
> *He frees himself who overcomes himself.*

According to the commentary which Goethe wrote for it in 1816, the finished poem would have shown that all the best men from all the ends of the earth can be gathered together here 'where each one reveres God according to his own mode.' All religions are valid if they recognize the sacred character of being. Goethe, like Herder, held that it was possible to love both Christ and Spinoza, and in 1785 he wrote to Jacobi, who had attacked the latter: 'You acknowledge that higher reality which is the basis of the whole of Spinozism, on which everything else rests and from which everything else flows. He does not prove the existence of God, existence is God. And if, because of this, others call him an atheist, I would call him *theissimus*, and even *christianissimus*, and praise him as such.'

But it is easy to see that this is a Christianity far removed from Christ. If nature is not absolutely identical with God, it is at least by her that He manifests Himself. She translates the divine attributes for our contemplation. In the hymn dated 1783, even if it was written by someone else after talking with Goethe, we can find Goethe's thought during these years:

Nature! She enfolds and embraces us. We are unable to escape from her and powerless to penetrate more deeply into her. Without asking us, without warning us, she draws us into the cycle of her dance and sweeps us with her until, exhausted, we escape from her arms.

Ah ma chère quel contretemps ! Le Duc a changé
de plan et nous ne partirons qu'en 8 jours.
J'en serois assez content, car il y a encore
toutes sortes de choses à voir ici. et nous connoissons
mieux notre monde; en partant, si ça n'étoit
pas ce terrible ma heure qu'il faut passer
(tout les jours à table).

Aujourd'hui, nous avons fait un tour forcé
pour voir la galerie de l'Abbadeu il y a de
très belles choses que je souhaiterois de
voir surtout un Everdingen
(m avec for

Je finis par un vers allemand) qui vera place)
dans f le (Poeme) que) je cheris tant, parceque) ff pourra
parler de toi, de mon) amour pour toi sous mille
formes sans que personne) (Kenkende) que toi veule)

Gewis) ich waere schon) so feine feine
Sowol die Welt nur offen liegt gegangen)
Bezwungen) mich) nicht übermaechtge Keine)
Die mein Geschik an deines angehangen
Daß ich in dir nun erst mich kennen lerne)
Kein Dichten, Trachten, Hoffen und Verlangen)
Allein nach Dir und Deinem Wesen draengt
Mein Leben nur an Deinem Leben haengt

ce 28 D'aout 1784

...She brings her creatures gushing out of nothingness, and says nothing to them of whence they come or where they go. They have only to go on, she knows their road.

... Everything is ever-present in her. She is unaware of the past as of the future. For her the present is eternity. She is good. I praise her with all her works.

...It is she who has set me here, it is she also who will lead me hence. I abandon myself to her. She can make what she will of me. She cannot hate her own work...

In order to make a better job of his administrative work, Goethe had applied himself more and more methodically to the natural sciences. He studied botany and mineralogy, took up drawing again, and studied anatomy with Professor Loder of Jena. On the 27th of March 1784 he wrote what reads like a proclamation of victory to Herder: 'I have found—neither gold nor silver, but what gives me an inexpressible joy: the intermaxillary bone in man.... You ought also to rejoice over this with all your heart, for it is as it were the key-stone of man's arch. It is not lacking, it is there!'

The reason this discovery delighted him so much was that it had a bearing on philosophy and religion and confirmed his intuition. It is not by any detail of his physical structure that man is differentiated from animals, it is by his whole nature. He wrote an essay on this discovery. Shortly before, he had written a poem, 'The Divine,' whose first two stanzas proclaim the same theme:

> Let man be noble,
> Rich in help, and good!
> For this alone
> Sets him apart
> From all the creatures
> Which we know.
>
> Hail to those unknown
> Higher beings
> Whom we half-sense!
> Let man be like them,
> His example teach us
> Belief in them.

Yet sometimes we can discern other notes through the bustle of his work and the serenity of his love-song. He wrote to Kestner

Letter from Goethe to Frau von Stein, of the 23rd-24th of August 1784. He had gone to the court of the Duke of Brunswick with Karl August, who was even more bored there than himself. The poem which he mentions is "The Mysteries," never completed. The verse quoted here was not included in the final fragmentary version.

that, following the example of Frederick II, who devoted a few hours of each day to his flute, he occasionally allowed himself the exercise of his own talent. In April 1780 he wrote in his diary: '... I am like a bird taken in a snare; I feel that I have wings and they cannot be used.' His 'daemon' could not, in the long run, be satisfied with these tasks which were being imposed upon him: 'I was really born to be a writer...' (10th of August 1782). 'I was made to be a private person, and I do not understand how fate has managed to fit me into the administration of a state and the life of a princely family.' (17th of September 1782.)

Since becoming first minister, this same year, he had begun to live in a house in the town. The house by the Ilm, with its garden, was henceforward to be no more than a 'retreat.'

However often he stifled it, the need for escape could not always be held in: 'I could almost wish to escape for a change of air, but I cannot imagine myself separated from you,' he wrote to Frau von Stein on the 8th of December 1782. 'If I did not have you, I should go out into the wide world' (24th of December.)

In proportion to the passing of the years, his exasperation grew. 'I am revising *Werther*, and it still seems to me that the author was at fault in not shooting himself when he'd finished writing' (24th of June 1786). 'I say that anyone who attends to administration, not being a reigning prince, must be either a philistine, a rogue or a fool' (10th of July 1786).

What had he written during these ten years? Now that, with Herder's help, he was preparing a complete edition of his works, he was in a better position to draw up the balance-sheet. There were a considerable number of short poems, a few longer ones, 'The Triumph of Sensibility,' in which he made fun of Werther and himself, *Iphigenie* in prose, two acts of *Tasso*, 'Wilhelm Meister's Theatrical Mission'—a sketch for the future novel—and some operettas. But *Egmont*, *Faust*, 'The Mysteries' and *Elpenor* were still unfinished. Not only his official tasks, but the duchy itself was a weariness to him. His eyes, hungering for light, were tired at last of the grey skies and dingy hues of Weimar. He was looking for a new form of art which only the ancient world could give. Ever since his childhood Italy had been calling to him. His Mignon had already sung: 'Knowst thou the land...?' And for him Italy meant also Greece, the whole of the ancient world in one.

Was not even his 'marriage of souls' with Charlotte beginning to be a burden? 'I am no longer a single, independent being'

(28th of June 1784). 'No, my love for you is no longer a passion, it is a sickness which is dearer to me than health and of which I do not wish to be cured' (In French, 30th of August 1784). But ten years are a long stretch for one by whom change is reckoned the very condition of duration. On the eve of his departure, there is a letter which gives more than a glimpse of Charlotte's jealousy and of their arguments and quarrels, and also, no doubt, of the weariness resulting from an equivocal situation: 'Until now I have borne all kinds of things in silence, and I have desired nothing so ardently as to see our relationship established in such a way that no power whatever could do anything against it. Failing this, I do not wish to live near you, and would prefer to remain in solitude in the world to which I am now going.' (1st of September 1786.)

He was not running away from her as he had run from Annette, Friederike, the other Lotte, and Lili. He had no intention of severing himself from her forever, any more than from Karl August or the rest of his friends. He simply felt that the time for this journey had come.

But he did not tell her where he was going. Nor did he tell the Duke from whom he had asked and obtained indefinite leave: '... I am under a constraint to lose myself in parts of the world where I am entirely unknown; I am going alone, under an assumed name, and I have great hopes of this enterprise, which may seem a somewhat strange one.'

So it was Herr Johann Philipp Möller who left Carlsbad for Rome on the 3rd of September 1786 at four o'clock in the morning. Only Seidel, his agent, confidant and secretary, who stayed behind at Weimar, knew the goal of his journey: 'I have not breathed a word to anyone.... If anyone asks for me, say that I shall be returning soon.'

XI. The Italian Journey:
September 1786 to June 1788

The story of Goethe's time in Italy is known to us from the travel diary he kept for Frau von Stein, from his letters, and from his *Italienische Reise*, published in 1814-16, 1817, and 1829, based on various writings and letters of which many are no longer in existence.

After leaving Carlsbad, his carriage passed through Eger, Ratisbonne, Munich, Innsbruck, and over the Brenner. To occupy the long hours on the road and the solitary evenings at inns, Goethe had brought *Iphigenie* to transcribe into iambic verse; but at first he spent his time observing: he had eyes for everything —weather, landscape, type of soil, plants, animals. His tone is often, unconsciously, that of a school-boy on holiday: 'I feel as if I had been born and brought up here, and were coming back from whaling off Greenland. . . . I am like a bear from the northern mountains, but I mean to give myself the pleasure of growing gradually accustomed to the style of the country.' (11th of September, after leaving Trent.)

From Trent he went to Verona, Vicenza and Padua. By the end of the month he was at Venice:

Thus it was written upon my page in the book of fate that in 1786, on the twenty-eighth of September, at five o'clock by our time, I should first come out of the Brenta into the lagoons and set eyes on Venice, and that I should soon afterwards be walking about and exploring this wonderful island-city. . . . And so, thank God, Venice is no longer a mere word to me, no longer that mere empty name by which I, being the deadly enemy of all hollow husks of words, had so often been disquieted. . . (Diary).

On the 1st of November, from Rome:

Yes, at last I have arrived at this, the capital of the world! . . .

I flew, as it were, over the Tyrolean mountains. I have had a good look at Verona, Vicenza, Padua, and Venice, a passing one at Ferrara, Cento and Bologna, hardly any at Florence. My longing to get to Rome was so great, and was intensifying so much at every moment, that further delay was impossible and I stopped only three hours at Florence. Now I am here, and at peace, and, it seems to me, at peace for the rest of my life. For one may well say that it is the beginning of a new life when we see with our own eyes that whole which we have known partially, and deeply, by heart. I am now seeing all the dreams of my youth come to life; I am seeing in reality the first engravings which I can remember—my father had hung an entrance-hall with views of Rome—and everything that I have known for so long in paintings and drawings, engravings and woodcuts, plaster and cork models is now all here before me at once; wherever I go I find old acquaintances in a new world. Everything is as I had conceived it, and everything is new. I can say the same of my own observations and ideas. I have not had any entirely new thoughts; I have not discovered anything entirely strange; but all my old ones have become so clear, so vital and so coherent that they may well count as new. (To his friends at Weimar, 1st of November 1786.)

. . . Pardon me my secrecy and my, so to speak, underground journey. I hardly dared to say where I was going even to myself; even on the way here I was still afraid, and only beneath the Porta del Popolo did I feel assured of Rome. . . . During the last few years, this place had become a sort of disease of which I could only be cured by seeing it and being in it. I can now confess that by the end I could not look at a Latin book or a drawing of any part of Italy. My desire to see this land was much more than ripe. (To the Duke, 3rd of November 1786.)

Almost the only people he saw were artists, amongst whom were Angelika Kaufmann and Tischbein, who appointed himself his guide.

I have at last reached the goal of my desires, and I am living here in such clarity and peace as you, knowing me as you do, can imagine. My practice of seeing and absorbing all things as they are, my faithful care to let my eye be light, and my total dissociation from all pretentiousness are making me very happy in my tranquillity.

*Every day there is some new object worthy of note, every day brings
fresh images, great and strange, and a whole which can be thought
of and dreamt of for long, but never attained by the imagination. . . .
What gives me the deepest joy is the effect which I can already feel
in my soul: an interior solidity imprinted, so to speak, on the mind,
gravity without aridity, an essential stability combined with joy. I
feel I shall rejoice in the blessed consequences of this throughout
my life.* (To the Herders, 10th-11th of November 1786.)

He went to the Raphael Loggia, to Saint Peter's, to the Sistine
Chapel...

*I am so possessed by Michelangelo that nature itself is tasteless
after him, since I cannot see it with eyes as great as his...* (To his
friends at Weimar, 2nd of December 1786.)

I am recovering here, bit by bit, from my salto mortale, *and
studying rather than enjoying myself. Rome is a world, and it
would take years simply to become aware of it all. . . . You need
to be so to speak reborn, and you look back at the ideas you have*

103

The pyramid of Cestius. (Drawing by Goethe, 1788).

hitherto had as if they were baby-shoes.... This past year has been the most important in my life; whether I die now or live a while longer, in either case it has been good. (To the Herders, 13th of December 1786.)

I did indeed think that I should learn something true here, but I did not suppose that I should be required to go back to so low a place at school, and the more I have to deny myself the more glad I am. I am like an architect wishing to build a tower who has laid his foundations badly; he realizes it while there is still time, gladly demolishes what he has so far raised above ground, so as to make more certain of his base, and rejoices in anticipation over the surer solidity of his building. Having studied nature so zealously and thoroughly during these last years is a help to me where art is concerned. (To Frau von Stein, 29th-30th December 1786.)

I have been cured of a passion, a violent illness, so as to be able to begin again to enjoy life, and history, and poetry, and the art of antiquity, and I have material for elaboration and completion which will last for years... (To his friends at Weimar, 6th of January 1787.)

104

I possess only one existence, and this time I have staked the whole of it, and am still staking it. If I come out of it safe and sound, physically and spiritually, if my nature and mind and fortune succeed in overcoming this crisis, then I will make up to you a thousand times over anything that needs to be made up to you. If I succumb, then I succumb; in any case, without this I was no longer good for anything. (To Frau von Stein, 17th-20th January 1787.)

In February he was at Naples, and again interested in everything: the life of the people, the mineralogy, botany and zoology of the place. He climbed Vesuvius, and went dangerously close to the crater for the sake of more accurate observation. He went to Pompeii and Herculaneum, and crossed over to Sicily at the end of March. He thought about Tasso, and of a play about Nausicaa. Back at Naples, he communicated his ideas about Homer to Herder, and also a thought which had come to him in the gardens at Palermo:

As for Homer, it is as though a veil had fallen from my eyes. His descriptions and similes and so on strike us as poetical, but they are in fact unutterably natural, though delineated with a positively

105

*awe-inspiring purity and intensity. Even the most extraordinary of
his invented incidents has a naturalness which I had never felt before
as I did there, in the presence of the things he describes.... For
the first time I find that the Odyssey has become a living word.*

*I must also confide to you that I am very near the secret of the
genesis and organization of plants, and that it is the simplest thing
conceivable. Beneath this sky it is possible to make the most
perfect observations. Quite clearly and without any doubt I have
discovered the principal point, where the germ is to be found; and
I can already see all the rest as a whole, and only need to clarify
certain points. My primitive plant is becoming the weirdest creature
in the world, for which nature herself shall envy me. With this for
a model, and the key to it, it will then be possible to invent an endless
series of plants which will be consistent, i.e., which, even if they do
not actually exist, yet could exist and are not just the shadows and
fancies of painters and poets but have an interior truth and in-
evitability. The same law will apply to all other living beings.* (17th
of May 1787.)

*I have been truly re-born and renewed and utterly fulfilled... The
fashion of this world passes away, and I would like to concern
myself only with what consists of abiding relationships.* (Italienische
Reise, 23rd of August 1787.)

*These lofty works of art have been brought forth by men, like the
loftiest of nature's works, in accordance with true and natural laws.
Everything of arbitrary invention collapses; where necessity is,
there is God.* (Italienische Reise, 6th of September 1787.)

*I am working hard and contentedly and waiting on the future.
It becomes clearer to me every day that I was really born for poetry,
and that during the next ten years, while I can still work at the top
of my pitch, I ought to cultivate my talent and make something good
of it, since it was the fire of youth which enabled me to achieve much
with little study. My long stay in Rome will have given me the
advantage of abstaining from the practice of the plastic arts.*
(Italienische Reise, 22nd of February 1788.)

He left Rome at the end of April 1788:

*When I left, I experienced suffering of a peculiar nature. To be
leaving this capital of the world, without hope of return, after having
lived here for some time, results in a feeling which cannot be
translated into words.... The whole play* [Tasso] *is shot through
with the painful feelings of a passionate soul being dragged irresistibly
into an irrevocable exile. This state of mind did not leave me
throughout the journey.*

XII. Weimar: 1788 to 1792

> *A difficult readjustment – Christiane*
> *Vulpius – The 'Roman Elegies' – Break*
> *with Frau von Stein – New theories on art*
> *and scientific studies – The master of culture*
> *– Domestic happiness and moral solitude.*

  The Italian journey was a decisive turning point in Goethe's
life and work. The word 'rebirth' recurs constantly in his letters,
always with a note of joy. The following lines from one of the
'Roman Elegies,' written after his return, express by contrast the
nostalgia he was feeling:

> *O how happy I feel in Rome! when I think of the time*
> *When the grey of the day was around me, back in the north,*
> *Sad was the sky, and heavy the weight of it on my shoulders,*
> *Colorless, formless lay, around me weary, the world;*
> *And I, over myself, for my unsatisfied spirit*
> *Spying out gloomy roads, in contemplative silence sank.*
> *Now surrounding my brow shines light of more luminous aether:*
> *Phoebus the god is summoning forms and hues to come forth.*
> *Night shines brilliant with stars, and rings with a gentle singing,*
> *And the moonlight to me is brighter than northern day.*

Goethe had now found that inner equilibrium of which he had had only a precarious sense through his love for Frau von Stein. He returned to Weimar on the 18th of June 1788; he had then to readjust himself. Frau von Stein had taken his flight very badly. He had left her long without news, and it appears, from his replies, that she wrote sharply to him. In his letters to her from Rome, we sometimes find a reappearance of the passionate note of earlier years: 'Do not think of me as parted from you; nothing in this world could replace for me what I should lose in you...' (23rd of September 1786). 'I am bound to you by all the fibres of my being. The way my memories often tear at me is terrible...' (21st of February 1787). But she was not his, and the thought of this burned and gnawed at him.

But only for a time. The southern world of nature and the art of the City took full possession of him. Gradually her distant image faded. He tells in the *Italienische Reise* of the 'fair Milanese' whom he met at Castelgandolfo and who suddenly set his heart on fire. It was a pure and youthful love, with no sequel. But there is an unambiguous, very eighteenth-century account of an amorous adventure in a letter to the Duke dated February 1788. Was her name really Faustina, as he calls her in the 'Roman Elegies'? From that time to the end of his visit he wrote only once to Frau von Stein—a short and startlingly banal letter.

When he returned to Weimar he was nearly thirty-nine. The time for nostalgic sighings was past. Frau von Stein was forty-six; she was more ailing and melancholy than ever. Perhaps she did not even try to recapture him.

Four weeks after his return Goethe met a girl of twenty-three who had come bringing a petition on behalf of her brother. Her father, a small official, had died and left them in straits. She was working in an artificial flower factory.

Once she[1] appeared to me, a brown-faced maiden, whose hair
Fell, all dusky and rich, over her forehead and down,
Short curled her locks in ringlets around her small delicate neck...

Christiane Vulpius imposed no 'novitiate' upon him.

Do not, beloved, regret that you were so quick to surrender!
Trust me, no insolent thought nor lowly of you do I hold.
Manifold work the arrows of love; from some of them, grazing,
Poison steals within, bringing sickness for years to the heart.

Christiane Vulpius (Drawing by Goethe).

Others, mightily feathered, with barbs all freshly sharpened,
Pierce to the marrow at once, unerringly kindle the blood.
In the heroic age, when gods and goddesses loved,
Desire followed close on sight, enjoyment close on desire.

In this affair, the senses were certainly the first to speak; Goethe was never more thoroughly a 'pagan' than during these years. The note struck in the 'Roman Elegies' was scarcely to be heard again in his works. He mixed memories of Italy with present reality:

Glad now on classical soil feel an excitement of spirit;
Worlds of both past and present more loud, more alluringly speak.
Here I follow good counsel, browse through the works of the ancients,
Thumbing with busy hand, daily with fresh delight.
But all the length of my nights, Love gives me other business;
Learned but half though I be, yet I am doubly blessed.
And am I not still learning, the form of the lovely bosom

The Herders.

The Duchess Louise, wife of Karl August (Painting by Tischbein, 1795).

Thus exploring, and passing my hand down over the thighs?
Only then understand I the marble, compare and consider,
See with feeling eye, feel with a seeing hand...
Then when sleep overcomes her I lie there with manifold thoughts.
Often, indeed, in her arms I have composed my poems
And the hexameter's measure, softly, with fingering hand,
Counted upon her back...

We have restricted ourselves to those of the 'Roman Elegies' which Goethe included in his collected works, omitting those which were more secretly printed after his death, which defy conventional standards of decency.

He did, however, love Christiane with his new-born heart, and was soon to say so. Weimar exclaimed over the ducal Counsellor and his 'mamsell.' Frau von Stein was one of the last to hear, and was deeply wounded. Goethe replied to her with dignity. It was

111

chiefly because of her, he said, that he had not gone back to Italy with Herder and the dowager duchess, despite their pressing invitations... 'and at that very moment I had to hear it persistently repeated that I might very well have stayed away altogether, that I was taking no interest in anyone in any case, etc. And all this before there could be any question of a new relationship which appears to wound you so much. And what kind of relationship

is it? Who is made the poorer by it? Who claims the feelings that I give to the poor soul, the hours that I spend with her?' (1st of June 1789). He insists on his friendship for Fritz, for Herder, for herself, and on the pleasure it would be to him to converse with her on 'interesting subjects.' His second letter is firmer and more painful than the first: 'I have known no greater happiness than my trust in you, which was always unlimited; from the moment when I can no longer rely on it, I shall be a different man, and I shall change still more as time goes on.... Give me back your trust... take a natural view of this thing...' (8th of June 1789.)

But the break was complete. At first he kept Christiane in his house by the Ilm. There she bore him a son on the 25th of December 1789, and almost immediately afterwards she came to live with him in his house in Weimar. There were four more children, who died soon after birth.

His readjustment with the Duke was easier. Goethe was discharged from his official duties, but left his emoluments. He remained in charge only of cultural matters: museums, schools

112

Christiane Vulpius, by Lips (1791).

of art, the University of Jena and, from 1791 onwards, the ducal theatre.

The greatest effect of his Italian 'rebirth' was in his art. His only desire on the journey had been to see classical beauty—the works of antiquity and of the Renaissance. Nature had revealed to him the answer to the enigma which the Earth Spirit had once refused to Faust. Underlying the multiplicity of appearances there is one single type. Evolution, in the form in which he sensed it, presented the idea of harmony. Nature remained an object of veneration, but from henceforward he saw it as Spinoza did, acting according to eternal and necessary laws, 'so divine that divinity itself could not change them.' This is the theme which runs through all his scientific researches, and henceforward he sees it as also applicable to art: the poet ought to strive, like the classical writers, to rediscover that which is eternal and unalterable underlying the diversity of forms, to discard all strongly individual elements and replace character by type. In accordance with these principles, he revised *Iphigenie* and *Tasso*.

He went on working at the complete edition of his works, but the 'Roman Elegies' (1788-90), the 'Venetian Epigrams' (1790), the translation of the old Low German epic of Reynard the Fox (1793-4) and a few minor theatrical works comprise the whole of his literary output during the first years after his return. He devoted himself to a greater extent to scientific work, wrote on the morphology and metamorphosis of plants and on animal structure, and began his study of optics.

Those around him scarcely understood him any more. He was content to rule over a little kingdom of connoisseurs whom he had gathered round him to collaborate in his work as superintendent of the cultural affairs of the duchy: Moritz and Heinrich Meyer— art critics whom he had met in Italy—and the artists Bury and Lips. From 1791 to 1797 he held gatherings in his house on Fridays where the principal subject discussed was art. He became gradually estranged from his former friends, as much through his new theories on art as because of the circumstances of his private life. Only the duke and the Herders retained his confidence. We can sense that he was often sad and embittered. From Breslau, where the duke had taken him on a visit of military inspection, he wrote: 'I am homesick; I have nothing left to search for in this world' (21st of August 1790). 'There is nothing but rottenness and shabbiness everywhere, and I certainly shan't have a really pleasant moment until the night when I have supper with you and sleep with my dear girl. So long as you keep on loving me, and a few good people still care about me, and my girl is faithful, the child alive and the big stove drawing well, I have nothing else to wish for for the time being.' (To the Herders, 11th of September 1790.)

Still the same sensuality; but when the 'Roman Elegies' were finished, 'there is so to speak not another trace of that vein to be found in me.' He thought about the simple things which are all men's goods: his hearth and home, the woman whom he thought of as his wife, his child. This is a Goethe who is as far removed from Werther as from Olympus, a Goethe who is little known and little discussed. But such domestic happiness was not to the measure of his stature. The reason why he prized it so highly was that he felt spiritually very much alone.

Goethe, by Lips *(1791).*

XIII. The French Revolution

Efforts at impartiality - First reactions - 'Campaign in France' - Valmy - Disillusion- ment of German hopes - The siege of Mainz: 'Injustice and disorder.'

I could not be a friend to the French Revolution, [said Goethe to Eckermann on the 4th January 1824] *for its horrors were too near to me, revolting me daily and hourly, whereas its beneficial results were still unforeseeable. Nor could it be a matter of indifference to me when efforts were made to provoke artificially similar events in Germany to those which had, in France, been the consequence of a great necessity. But nor was I in any way a friend of arbitrary despotism. I was also perfectly convinced that no great revolution is ever the fault of the people, but always that of the government. Revolutions are absolutely impossible when governments are con- stantly just and vigilant, forestalling them by opportune reforms and not holding out to the very moment when what is needed is obtained by force from below.*

But because I hated revolutions I was called a friend of the estab- lished order. But that is an ambiguous title, which I wish to disclaim. If the established order were always excellent, good and just, I should not object. But since what is established includes, along with much that is good, much evil, injustice and imperfection, a friend of the established order is often in fact a friend of what is outworn and evil. But time is in the grip of perpetual progress, and human affairs take a new form every fifty years, so that an institution which was a perfect achievement in 1800 may well be defective by 1850.

We see here his constant desire for equity.

Goethe was never, in fact, on the side of the powerful against the weak. As an administrator, his aim was to alleviate the lot of the humble. Had he been younger, he would no doubt have been an enthusiastic supporter of the Revolution, as were his friends—contemporaries or seniors as they were—Herder, Wieland, Knebel and Stolberg, and, at a further remove, Klopstock and Bürger. But, leaving aside the consciousness he now had of all that he owed to his prince, his ideal at the time when the Revolution broke out was no longer that of *Sturm und Drang* but of harmony. The Revolution represented a disturbance of his conceptions, his strivings and his work. He tried at first to ignore it, to take refuge in science and in theories of art.

However, he loosed a few shafts at both sides in the 'Venetian Epigrams' (1790). He then began to comment on the events of the Revolution in a few plays which are by no means among his best works: *The Great Kophta* (1791), based on the diamond necklace affair; *The Citizen General* (1792), *The Infuriated* (1794) and *The Maid of Oberkirch* (1795), of which the two last remained only fragments. The *Conversations of German Emigrés* (1795) raised considerable discussion. In *Hermann und Dorothea* (1796–7), a masterpiece in the fullest sense, which has the French Revolution for its background, he had already succeeded in withdrawing enough from its events to form a judgment upon them. In *The Natural Daughter* (1799–1803), which was to have been the first play of a trilogy which he did not finish, the conflict between the old order and new ideas which lies at the origin of all revolutions is treated at the level of types.

Goethe became more involved in contemporary history than he would have wished. He felt he could not refuse when the duke, who commanded a regiment of Prussian cavalry, summoned him to camp at Praucourt, near Longwy. He accompanied the army, in an entirely non-professional capacity, from the 23rd of August to the end of October 1792, with his mind more preoccupied with optical theories than with military operations. It was a trying campaign, conducted under continual rain and over muddy roads. He took notes, and wrote up his memories in 1821, making use, for the general course of events, of books which had been published in the meanwhile. His work appeared with the title of *Campaign in France*. Here, dated 19th of September, are his famous lines on Valmy:

All this happened to a ceaseless accompaniment of thundering cannon... The sky was lit up by this terrific blasting, for the way they were using the cannon was exactly like volley-firing—not evenly, but alternately increasing and decreasing. At one o'clock in the afternoon, after a slight pause, it was at its most violent; the earth shook in the most literal sense, yet no slightest alternation could be seen in the positions. No one knew what the outcome would be.

...Thus the day had passed; the French stood fast and immovable, and Kellermann had taken up a more favorable position; our men were withdrawn from the firing line, and it was just as though nothing had happened. Consternation spread through the army. That morning, everyone had thought we had the French on toast and were about to make one mouthful of them; unquestioning confidence in such an army and in the Duke of Brunswick had persuaded even me to take part in this dangerous expedition; but now everyone was going his own way, without interchange of glances—or, if there were, they called forth only curses and maledictions. It happened that just as night fell we had formed into a circle, where we could not even, as normally, light a fire in the center; most of us were silent, a few were talking, and none with sense or judgment. At least someone called out to know what I thought about it? For I had been in the habit of cheering and enlivening the party with brief observations. This time I said: 'From this day and this place there begins a new age in world history, and you will be able to say that you were there.'

The victorious French went on into Germany. There is a passage in *Hermann und Dorothea* (Canto VI), which describes the hopes of the Rhinelanders and the cruel disillusionment which followed:

Did not all peoples together, then in the days of the tumult,
Look to the capital city, as long it had been, of the world, as
Now more deserving than ever to bear that glorious title?
Were not the names of the men who first declared us that message
Equal to all the highest set under the stars of heaven?...
And, as neighbors, the first were we to be keenly enkindled.
Then began the war, and columns of arms-bearing Frenchmen
Drawing nearer; but still they seemed to bring nothing but friendship.
And they brought it indeed: for all were exalted in spirit
And with delight they planted the joyous saplings of freedom,
Promising unto each his own, and to each self-rule.

117

High was the jubilation of youth, and the joy of old age,
Merrily then the dance began around the new standard.
So did they quickly win, these overmastering Frenchmen,
First the souls of the men with the fire of their glad beginnings,
Then the hearts of the women with irresistible charm...
But the sky was soon overcast. For the summit of power
Struggled a breed corrupt, unfit to achieve any good thing.
They began murdering each other, began oppressing their new
Neighbors and brothers, and sending out to us crowds of self-seekers.
Riotously lived the great ones among them, plundering us greatly,
Plundered and rioted too, even to the lowest, the low.
Each seemed only concerned lest something be left for the morrow.
All too great was distress, and daily oppression grew greater:
No one would hear our lament, for they were the lords of the moment.
Even on minds resigned then came there sorrow and anger;
Each thought only, and swore, the wrongs of all to avenge
And the most bitter loss of a hope thus doubly betrayed.
Then was fortune changed, and swung to the side of the Germans,
And the Frenchman fled in forced marches hastily back.
Ah, then first did we feel the tragic fortune of warfare!
For the victor is great and good; or at least he appears so...
But the fugitive knows no law, seeking but to avoid death...

After the Valmy campaign, Goethe went back by Luxembourg
and Trier, and by boat down the Moselle to Coblentz and down the
Rhine to Düsseldorf. He spent some time at Pempelfort with his
friends the Jacobis and then at Münster with Princess Galitzin.
He did not return to Weimar until December 1792, via Paderborn
and Cassel.

By the 27th of May he had rejoined the Duke of Weimar at the
headquarters of the Prussian armies. From the 16th of June the
city of Mainz was under siege and bombardment. On the 22nd of
July the leaders of both armies decided that the capitulation
should be carried out on the following day. As soon as the in-
habitants learned the news they began trying to get back into their
city, and sentries had to be doubled to prevent them. On the 23rd,
the Allies occupied the outworks. Goethe made a tour round the
outside of the town in his carriage, and met a citizen of Mainz
who asked him to take his son with him because the child was tired.
The man was swearing death and destruction to the *Klubisten*,
the Germans who had come to terms with the French, either from
conviction or, more often, from self-interest.

I spoke propitiatory words to him, pointing out that the return to

Night bombardement of Mainz,
by the Frankfurt painter Schütz.

peaceful domestic conditions must not be sullied by fresh civil war, hatred and vengeance, or misfortune would have no end. The punishment of such as were guilty must be left to the Allied leaders and to the lawful ruler of the country after his return.

There were difficulties which delayed the departure of the French garrison, and the citizens learnt, to their fury, that some of the *Klubisten* had eluded the vigilance of the sentries and escaped. On the 24th of July Goethe watched the departure of the occupation troops from a window, with his friend Gore, an Englishman living at Weimar who had come with him.

There were Prussian cavalry leading the way, followed immediately by the French garrison. It was a procession of an aspect as strange as anything could be: a column of Marseillais, small, black-haired and dressed in tattered clothes of all colors tramped past, looking as though King Edwin had flung open his mountain and sent forth an army of nimble dwarfs. Then followed more regular troops, looking stern and bitter but by no means downcast or ashamed. But what must have affected everyone as the most striking sight of all was the ride past of the mounted chasseurs. They had come up level with us in complete silence, and then their music struck up the Marseillaise. That Te Deum of the Revolution always has something of tragedy and foreboding about it, however cheerfully it is performed; but on this occasion they took it at a very slow tempo, in time with the creeping pace at which they were riding. It was a moving, a terrible and a solemn sight to see the riders come up—tall, lean men in middle life, the expressions on their faces matching the sounds of their music: taken one by one, they might have been likened to Don Quixote, in the mass they seemed worthy of all honor.

On the 25th, Goethe recorded with chagrin that steps had not been taken to prevent disorder, which had become all the more necessary because of the steady increase in popular indignation. Suspected vehicles were stopped, and one *Klubist* so discovered was beaten up. Some of the girls of Mainz, bent on following their lovers, were found mixed up with the foot-soldiers, calling forth appropriate comments. The women, in particular, were convinced that the French soldiers were carrying off with them things they had found in the citizens' houses. In the midst of all this, a man came by on horseback, and with him a very pretty girl dressed as a man. There was a moment's silence, and then a sudden cry: 'Stop him! Kill him! It's that scoundrel of an architect who first looted the Cathedral deanery and then set fire to it!'

It happened near the ducal headquarters. Seeing the possibility of an outbreak, Goethe thought of the Duke of Weimar coming back to find a mass of wreckage piled before his door. He harangued the mob, reminding them that the king had promised free egress to all, that onlookers had no right to be anything but peaceable, and that their misfortunes and hatred did not entitle them to take any action. A few of the bolder spirits still pressed forward. Goethe recognized the man he had met the previous evening, and specially exhorted him to keep calm. There was a moment of indecision, and then the crowd fell back, impressed. The threatened *Klubist* thanked Goethe and went on with the 'lovely girl.'

Gore was astonished, and asked Goethe, in his mixture of English and French: 'What fly stings you? You pushed yourself into an affair which might have gone ill.' Goethe asked in return what good purpose would have been served, except to set them in a rage, by letting the crowd pillage the man's baggage-wagons? If he had got quietly off with ill-gotten goods, so much the worse.

. . . My good Gore could not be content that I should have dared so much, at my own risk, for an unknown and possibly criminal individual. I kept pointing out to him, jokingly, how clean the square was in front of the house, and at last I said impatiently: 'It's just part of my nature: I would rather do something unjust than suffer a disorder.'

The authenticity of many historic sayings is disputed. Even though it is he himself who quotes them, Goethe's words at Valmy are no exception to this, on the grounds that he reported them thirty years after the event. But the sentence on injustice and disorder, spoken one year later, is recorded in the *Siege of Mainz*, which was written at the same period as the *Campaign in France*. Why, then, has French opinion decreed such a destiny for the second of these sayings, and given it a meaning which it did not have? For 'disorder' here meant a riot, with all its consequences; the 'injustice' of which he was guilty was to prevent popular vengeance from being taken on a man who *may* have been guilty, and therefore *may* have been innocent. What would have been said of Goethe if he had let the man be murdered before his eyes, without interfering?

But it is precisely the most unjust legends which have the strongest hold on life.

XIV. Friendship with Schiller: 1794 to 1805

> *Initial antipathy* – Die Horen – *The decisive meeting – 'A second spring...' – Classicism – Various activities –* Amyntas – *Schiller's death.*

There was certainly something daemonic presiding over my relationship with Schiller; we might have been brought together earlier or later, but that we were so just at the time when I had the Italian journey behind me and Schiller was beginning to tire of philosophical speculation was important, and full of consequences for both of us. (To Eckermann, 24th of March 1829.)

He wrote elsewhere that his relationship with Schiller was the happiest of all the events which fortune had kept in store for his maturity.

Schiller's first successes had been won in Goethe's absence. Now that Weimar was the most important center of culture in Germany, he had left his friends in Leipzig to come and live there. He had gradually established himself, but it irritated him to be surrounded by constant talk of Goethe, and when the latter returned from Italy things were no better: he felt that Goethe was in his way, and, by this own admission, felt for him 'a strange mixture of love and hatred.' As for Goethe:

After my return from Italy, where I had striven to develop a greater precision and purity in every branch of art, without paying any attention to what was going on in Germany at the same time, I found that certain literary works, both new and old, were much in favor...

Amongst them, he thought Schiller's *The Robbers* particularly detestable, 'because here a vigorous but immature talent had been

123

pouring over our country an impetuous flood of those very paradoxes, ethical and dramatic, from which I had been striving to purify myself.'

He was so disturbed by it that he even thought of abandoning poetry altogether. Moreover, Schiller's philosophical speculations alien as they were to his own realist position, put him off even more. In spite of being neighbors, they met only rarely in the houses of mutual friends. In 1789 Goethe arranged for Schiller to be given a chair at the University of Jena, partly in order to be of service to him but also for the sake of the distance it put between them.

Six years went by. Goethe continued to ignore Schiller, and the latter felt deeply humiliated. However, at the end of June 1794 he wrote Goethe a letter couched in the most elaborate diplomatic terms to ask for his collaboration in the review, *Die Horen*, which he was founding. And Goethe accepted 'gladly and with all his heart.'

They both belonged to the same society for natural science in Jena. The following July they came away from one of its meetings together, and fell into discussion. Schiller expressed the opinion that such a fragmentary manner of presenting nature was not calculated to encourage the layman.

I replied that it was perhaps uncongenial even to the initiate, and that there might surely be another way to approach nature—not piecemeal, in isolated fragments, but presenting it in its living activity, trying to work outwards from the whole to the parts. He wanted further explanation of this, but made no secret of his doubts; he could not admit that anything of the sort could, as I maintained, be the product of experience itself.

We arrived at his house, and our discussion induced me to go in; there I gave him a lively account of the metamorphosis of plants, conjuring up a symbolic plant, with characteristic strokes of the pen, before his eyes. He took it all in, and watched with great attention and a thorough grasp of the matter; but when I had finished he shook his head and said: 'That's not an experience, it's an idea.' I was pulled up short, and somewhat annoyed; for this was to give the strongest possible statement of the point of division between us . . . My former dislike stirred again, but I pulled myself together and said: 'Well, I am delighted to be having ideas without knowing it, and seeing them with my very eyes.'

The discussion continued, Schiller confronting Goethe with Kantian philosophical arguments. Neither could claim the victory. 'But the first step had been taken.' A few days later Schiller

wrote Goethe his famous letter of the 23rd of August 1794, in which he made an amazingly penetrating analysis of his genius. Goethe was surprised and delighted, and replied with enthusiasm:

You yourself will soon see how very beneficial your interest in me is going to be to me; for as you get to know me better you will discover in me a sort of obscurity and hesitancy which I cannot master, clearly aware of it as I am. (27th of August 1794.)

Goethe then invited Schiller to spend a fortnight with him, so that they could draw up a common intellectual balance-sheet and explain their plans to each other. They found that their aesthetic theories had converged. Traveling by different roads—for the one

125

Goethe about 1792-5.
(Life-size watercolor by Meyer).

it had been the study of nature and the experience of Italy, for the other it had been philosophical speculation—they had arrived at the same norm, and their daily intercourse henceforth permitted them to give it an ever more precise form: a noble ideal of humanity, most perfectly embodied for them, who saw with Winckelmann's eyes, in the Greeks.

It is impossible to say which of them received most in the exchange. Schiller, who was just ten years younger than Goethe, benefited from his elder's wider experience of the world and of men, from his more spontaneous genius and from his truly universal culture. Goethe, who had been in danger of letting himself be swallowed up by his scientific studies, recovered his delight in literary work, was introduced to Kantian philosophy, came in contact with the younger set in Jena, and made some approach —though cautiously—to the Romantic movement. Most important of all, he had henceforth a friend who could read his work, including even the scientific essays, with a spirit both of sympathy and of criticism which was useful to him without irritating him —or, at least, only very rarely. 'For me, especially, it was a second spring, with everything coming merrily to bud at once.'

Goethe's abundant correspondence and his *Annalen*—a continuation of the memoirs—keep us informed of their activities. Since his years in Frankfurt Goethe had never done so much work and produced so much as during these eleven years. Schiller the fighter first induced him to collaborate with him in loosing off the barbed distiches of the *Xenien* (1795–6), aimed at their common adversaries. As director of the Weimar theatre he took pains with the production of its repertory, more especially when he introduced Schiller's trilogy on Wallenstein to the public. He began work on an *Achilleis*, wrote *The Natural Daughter*, and, with his friend Meyer, published an art review, *Propyläen*. At the same time he busied himself with insects, plants and chemistry. He performed a mass of experiments on light, convinced that Newton was wrong, that colors are not due to the splitting of white light but to the greater or lesser intensity of light. In the eyes of posterity, these are side-issues to his work; not for himself, however: he always gave himself wholly to whatever he was doing. However, Schiller, with proper discernment, used his good influence to urge him to resume work once more on *Wilhelm Meister* and *Faust*.

In 1797 *Hermann und Dorothea* appeared. The idyllic story stands out in relief, in all its fresh simplicity, against the background of the French Revolution. Its sympathetic presentation of the German petty bourgeoisie, with their wisdom and industry and true humanity, won back for Goethe the popularity which he had in some measure lost while producing works too directly inspired by Greek classicism. Despite the difficulty of its hexameters, *Hermann und Dorothea* was Goethe's greatest success since *Werther*.

This was the year of the ballads, during which Schiller wrote his most famous ones. Goethe's contribution was 'The Sorcerer's Apprentice,' 'The God and the Bayadere,' and 'The Bride of Corinth,' a protest against the Christian ideal on behalf of paganism. This was also the year of his great elegies in classical form: 'Euphrosyne,' on the death of a young actress, 'Alexis und Dora,' and 'The New Pausias and his Flower-girl,' in which he portrayed Christiane.

In Switzerland, whence he returned for the third time in 1797, he conceived the idea of another elegy, 'Amyntas,' which he sent to Schiller on the 25th of November. The latter discreetly congratulated him on having used such simple means to make it so deeply moving and so highly significant. We can only guess at the conversations of which it is an echo. Goethe still loved Christiane, with a love which had begun with his senses and then taken possession of his heart. She was, moreover, a good person and a good housekeeper, but he, better than anyone, was aware of her lack of culture and her many deficiencies. Physically, she had not yet become the 'giddy-pated sausage' whom Bettina von Arnim was to make the butt of her malicious tongue, but she was growing stout, losing her charm, was rather too much addicted to dancing and inferior company, while her cumbersome family used to invade the great house. Goethe, who hated noise, used to take refuge at Jena, travel, or go to watering-places. Perhaps Schiller, who had made an honorable marriage, has expressed surprise to Goethe over his entanglement with her.

Do not wrinkle your brow yet deeper, my friend; listen gently.
Hear what I yesterday learnt from a tree, down there by the brook.
Apples but few it bears for me now, that was once heavy laden;
See, the guilt is the ivy's, which strongly entwines it around.
And I grasped my knife, with its blade curved crooked and sharpened,
Severed and slashed and tore, trailer by trailer it fell;
All at once, though, I shuddered, as, deeply and piteously sighing,
Out of the topmost boughs issued a whispered lament:
O thus injure me not! your loyal garden-companion,
Many delights you owed me, long ago, as a boy.

127

GOETHE, *by* BURY (*1800*).

CHRISTIANE VULPIUS, BY BURY (*1800*).

O thus injure me not! Along with this tangle of trailers
Which you destroy with violence, you tear my life out of me.
Have I myself not nourished her, tenderly trained her upon me?
Are not her leaves to me as near akin as my own?
Shall I not love this plant, which, in need of me only,
Quietly entwines herself, with hungry strength, round my side?
Thousands of shoots have rooted, with thousands on thousands of
[fibres
Deep she has plunged herself into the stuff of my life.
Nourishment from me she takes; that which I need, she enjoys now,
Yes, and the marrow of me she sucks, and sucks out my soul.
                                    ...And my loftiest branches
Wither, and withers already the bough stretched over the brook ...
Her alone do I feel, embracing me, joy in my fetters...
Do thou withhold thy knife, O Nikias, spare a poor being
Willingly forced to ruin himself in a loving delight!
Sweet is all prodigal spending. O this, its sweet best, let me savor!
He who entrusts him to love, will he take thought for his life?

The privations of poverty which he suffered in his youth had left
Schiller in delicate health. Goethe, on his side, had undergone a
severe crisis in 1801, beginning with a chill, which had brought
him close to death. At the beginning of 1805 they both fell ill and
were unable to see each other or communicate except by short
notes. Goethe began slowly to recover, whereas Schiller's illness
grew worse. He died on the 9th of May. No one dared to tell
Goethe until he himself put the question to Christiane, and understood.

His grief was very great. 'I thought it was myself I should lose,
and I lose a friend, and, in him, the half of my own existence'. (To
Zelter, 1st of June 1805). As always, he sought consolation in
work. Schiller had left an unfinished play, *Demetrius*. They had
discussed it together so much that it was all present to his mind.

I now burned with the desire to continue our intercourse in defiance
of death, to preserve his ideas, views and intentions in every detail...
The loss of him seemed restored, if I could continue his existence...
But obstacles stood in the way of carrying out this plan:

... They might have been set aside with a little prudence and wisdom,
but in the passionate impetuosity and confusion I was in I only in-
creased them... I was gripped by unbearable suffering, and since
my physical ills separated me from all society, I was seized by the
most wretched loneliness. My diaries record nothing of that time:
their blank pages are a sign of the emptiness of my state...

XV. Wilhelm Meister's Apprenticeship

Between 1777 and 1785 Goethe had written *Wilhelm Meister's Mission in the Theatre*. It is likely that, but for Schiller's encouragement, the novel would have remained unfinished, as did so many of his works. *Wilhelm Meister* engrosses a considerable share of the letters between the two friends, and it is plain from these letters that the same applies to their conversations.

The *Theatralische Sendung* was recovered only in 1910. The beginning of the final work can, in its main lines, be discerned in it. Young Meister, a merchant's son, goes on a business journey for his father's firm. He falls in with some strolling players, joins them, and acts in the company at a castle where they find admittance. Afterwards, their encampment is attacked by robbers. Wilhelm is wounded, and his life is saved by some unknown benefactors amongst whom is a fair Amazon whom he cannot forget. Shakespeare's plays lie at the heart of the novel. Wilhelm's great desire is to put on a perfect production of *Hamlet*. At the moment when his wish seems about to be granted, the novel in its original form breaks off.

The *Theatralische Sendung* is full of Goethe's vitality, his impulse to write for the joy of writing. Situations are multiplied, characters abound: we need mention only Mignon and the Harper.

But when Goethe took up his work again, he altered the whole story. Even the primary intention was changed. It is no longer chance which leads Wilhelm from one experience to the next but a sort of Masonic brotherhood, into which he is not to be initiated until much later. Goethe gave free rein to his delight in mystification and disguise. Wilhelm receives aids and signs and warnings which create an atmosphere of mystery round his love-affairs and adventures in the theatre and elsewhere. The aim of the Company of the Tower is to discover men of worth and form them into an élite fit for action. It works on the principle of leaving them to follow their own inclinations; once they have realized that they have gone wrong, it is all the easier for them to find their way back to the right road.

The more noble of the feminine characters whom Goethe here presents are not willing to accept this Rousseauesque method of pedagogy. Book VI consists of the 'Confessions of a Beautiful Soul,' in which the lofty figure of Fräulein von Klettenberg lives again. This 'beautiful soul' does not agree that the best way to cure children of their inclinations is to let them start by abandoning themselves to them: 'I hope that this strange experiment may succeed; with natures as good as theirs, it is perhaps possible.' As one who owes all her moral foundation to Christianity, and lives only by her faith, she suffers at seeing 'that they try to remove everything from the children which might lead them to communion with themselves and with that Invisible who is the one and only true Friend.'

As for Natalie, the 'fair Amazon' whom he meets again and who is also concerned with education, Wilhelm asks her:

'Then do you too leave each person's own nature to achieve its own development? Do you too allow those who belong to you to search, to go astray, to make blunders and either happily to find their goal or unhappily to lose themselves in error?'

'No,' said Natalie, 'that fashion of dealing with people would be entirely contrary to my mind... To me it seems necessary to set forth certain rules and impress them on children, so as to put something definite and steady into their lives.'

'If we take people simply as they are, we make them worse; if we treat them as if they were what they ought to be, then we bring them to the point to which they were meant to be brought.'

Wilhelm perceives that he was mistaken in making the theatre his aim, and feels that he has wasted his life; but he has nevertheless learnt through his experiences. In the course of his initiation, he is given his 'articles of apprenticeship.' After curing him of his error, the Company brings him to realize a further priciple: 'Man cannot

be happy until he himself sets limits to his indeterminate striving.'
He achieves his true value through integration into the social order.
'It is well for him to learn to live for others, and to forget himself
in doing his duty.' 'I am leaving the theatre,' writes Wilhelm, 'to
associate myself with men whose intercourse will certainly lead me
to what is in every sense a purer and more assured activity.' He
intends to use part of his fortune to buy some land and develop it
in collaboration with his friends.

It gives a false impression of the book, however, to try to disentangle its main ideas. First and foremost, Goethe was a
creative story-teller. He romances over all his innumerable in-
trigues and their solutions. The child Mignon, whose song was
once the symbol or his own longing for Italy, dies of her love for
Wilhelm. The Harper, who has read the mystery of her fate, cannot bear it, and kills himself. Wilhelm first asks in marriage the
hand of the practical Therese, an idealized version of Christiane
Vulpius, but before it is too late he grows aware of his love for
Natalie, the most perfect which he has ever known. There is a
further joy in store for him: the Company reveals to him that the
little boy to whom he has given his heart is his own son by the
actress Mariane.

Schiller wanted the philosophical idea of the novel to be
brought out more clearly. Goethe stood on his rights as an artist.
He said years later to Eckermann:

*People look for some central point, which is difficult and not even
a good thing. I should think that a rich and manifold life passing
before our eyes is something in itself, without any explicit purpose,
which refers only, after all, to the idea. But if you must have something of the sort, stick to the words which Friedrich speaks to the
hero at the end: 'You seem to me like Saul the son of Kish, who went
out to look for his father's asses and found a kingdom.' Stick to that.
For the whole work seems to be saying, fundamentally, no more than
this—that man, despite all his follies and confusions, is led by a
higher hand and does reach a happy goal.*

Faust with Gretchen and Mephistopheles with Frau Marthe
(Engraving by Tony Johannot).

XVI. Faust

As far back as 1790 Goethe had published *Faust: ein Fragment*, containing some additions to the *Urfaust* of 1773-75 and stopping short after the funeral of Gretchen's mother. Urged by Schiller, he returned to the work in 1797, and wrote the dedication and the two prologues. He then stopped, and it was not till 1806 that he finished the First Part, which was published in 1808.

From now on, the play takes on the proportions of a cosmic poem. The 'Prologue in Heaven,' a dialogue between the Lord and Mephistopheles, presents the problem of good and evil and freedom. Is Faust, as a second Job and representative of the human soul, to let himself be seduced by the powers of evil, or will the Lord have the last word?

MEPHISTOPHELES: *The godling of the world's of the same stamp as*
[*always,*
And just as queer as on the first of days.
He'd be a little better at living
But for that gleam of heaven's light you give him;
He calls it reason, and its only use is
To make him beastlier than any brute is.
Saving Your Grace's presence, he seems to me
Like one of those long-legged crickets to be,
That flies and flies in flying springs
But in the same old grass the same wee tune still
[*sings.*
And if he'd only stick to lying in grasses!
He shoves his nose in everything that's nasty.

THE LORD: *And hast thou nothing more to say to me?*
Dost thou still come for naught but to accuse?
Is there on earth naught that seems good to thee?

MEPHISTOPHELES: *No, Lord! I find it, frankly, there, as always, bad.*
I'm sorry for the humans and their misery of
[*living;*
Poor things, I've not the heart to plague them,
[*even.*

THE LORD: *Dost thou know Faust?*
MEPHISTOPHELES: *The Doctor?*
THE LORD: *He is my servant.*

135

MEPHISTOPHELES: *Indeed! He serves by some peculiar rule!*
No earthly meat or drink suffices for that fool!
His inner ferment drives him out afar,
He's partly conscious of how mad he is;
From heaven he demands each fairest star
And all the best, too, of each earthly bliss,
And all that's near and all that's far
Cannot content that deep-stirred heart of his.

THE LORD: *Though now he serves me but confusedly*
I will soon lead him out into the light.
The gardener knows, seeing leaves on the young
                                               [tree,
That flowers and fruit will future years delight.

MEPHISTOPHELES: *What will you wager? You shall lose him yet,*
If you will only give me leave
Gently upon my road his feet to set!

THE LORD: *So long as still on earth he lives*
It still is not forbidden thee.
For man must wander all the while he strives.
. . . Well, be it as thou wilt!
Lure, if thou canst, this spirit from his true source
And lead him, if thou seize him in thy grip,
With thee upon thy downward course—
And stand ashamed, if thou at last must say:
A good man, in the dark still pressing on,
Is well aware of which is the right way.

MEPHISTOPHELES: *Well and good! Only, it won't last long.*
I've no fears for my wager, none whatever.
When I've accomplished my endeavor
Then you must let me triumph to my fill.
Dirt shall he eat, and with a will,
Even as the serpent, my notorious cousin!

THE LORD: *. . . Too apt to slumber are man's energies,*
Unchanging rest he grows too soon to love;
I gladly, then, this comrade let him have
Who stings, stirs, and creates, though devil-wise.

Mephistopheles defines himself later on as 'the spirit which forever denies,' but also as 'a part of that power which forever wills
evil and forever creates good.' We must remember that Goethe in
his youth had drawn away from the Pietists because he could not
agree with them in acknowledging a radical corruption in human

138

nature. It is in *Faust* that this optimistic view finds its finest expression, and here it links up with the traditional theological thesis that the desire of a soul which no earthly joy can appease is an unconscious appeal to the abundance of God.

After his disappointment in the apparition of the Earth Spirit, Faust is tempted to suicide. The ringing of bells and changing of hymns for Easter Morning, which remind him of his childhood faith, inspire him to throw away the poisoned cup. During his Easter Morning walk with Wagner, the simple joy awakened in men of all classes by the first breath of spring contrasts with his melancholy yearning.

> *See there, how in a glow of evening sun*
> *The green-embowered cottages are shining!*
> *He presses on, and fades; the day is past;*
> *Yonder he hastes, in quest of life renewed.*
> *No wings, alas, to raise me from the ground,*
> *That I might strive and strive again to follow!*
> *I'd see in the unending rays of evening*
> *The quiet world there lying at my feet,*
> *With every peak on fire, and every vale at peace,*
> *The silver brook flowing in golden streams.*
> *Nor would my godlike course be hindered then*
> *By the wild mountain-range with all its gorges;*
> *The sea already, with warm-water inlets,*
> *Lies open now to my astonished eyes.*
> *Yet seems the god to sink away at last;*
> *But there awakens now fresh impulse in me;*
> *I hasten on to drink his endless light,*
> *The day before me and the night behind,*
> *The sky above me and the waves below.*
> *A lovely dream to dream while he declines.*
> *Alas, thus easily to wings of spirit*
> *Bodily wings come not to be conjoined!*
> *And yet it is inborn in every man*
> *To feel a longing urge both up and onward*
> *When high above us, lost in that blue space,*
> *The lark her warbling song is singing . . .*
> *. . . There dwell two souls, alas, within my breast,*
> *And each desires to sever from the other:*
> *The one, in sturdy longing after love*
> *Holds fast with clinging organs to the world;*

> The other strives with power from the dust
> To rise to our high forbears' fields afar.
> O, if there be here spirits of the air,
> Who rule and weave your webs twixt earth and
> [heaven,
> Descend from out that golden mist, and lead me
> Hence to new life of many-changing hues!

Faust, by that profound intuition which is the divine spark within him, knows that though the evil spirit may well provide him with cheap pleasures, he will never be able to satisfy what is best in his soul:

> If ever I lie down in peace upon a bed of sloth,
> Then let me there and then be lost!
> If ever thou canst flatteringly delude me
> That I take pleasure in myself,
> If ever thou canst with enjoyment fool me,
> Let that day be the last for me!
> I lay the wager!

MEPHISTOPHELES: *Done!*

FAUST: *And done again!*

> If I shall to the moment say:
> Stay yet awhile! Thou art so fair!
> Then shalt thou rivet me in chains,
> Then will I gladly be struck down!
> Then may the death-bell toll for me,
> Then art thou of thy service free,
> The clock may stop, the hand may fall,
> Time for me shall be no more.
> ...Hear this: of joy there is no question here!
> To frenzy am I vowed, to savor of pain,
> The lover's hatred, chagrin's stimulant.
> My breast, from yearning after knowledge healed,
> Henceforth shall never close itself to pain,
> And all that falls as lot to all mankind
> I mean to savor deep within myself,
> Seize with my spirit all its heights and depths,
> Its weal and woe heap up upon my heart,
> And so enlarge myself to be man's self
> And, like man's self, at last to shipwreck too!

After his meeting with Gretchen, Faust leaves her in an attempt to escape from temptation. He seeks to recover his better soul in solitude, through the contemplation of nature. This passage, written after his return from Italy, is a hymn addressed by Goethe to the Earth Spirit who has at last, through scientific laws, revealed to him some of his secrets.

> *Exalted Spirit, you have given me all,*
> *All that I asked, you gave. And no: in vain*
> *You turned your face upon me from the fire.*
> *You gave me glorious nature for a kingdom,*
> *And power to feel and taste her. Not alone*
> *A cold, astonished audience with her granted*
> *But gave me leave to gaze within her breast*
> *Deeply, as in the bosom of a friend.*
> *You lead the ranks of living things before me*
> *And teach me thus to know my brothers here*
> *In silent bush, and in the air and water.*
> *When through the forest tempest roars and snarls,*
> *The giant fir tree, falling, neighbor trunks*
> *And neighbor branches smashes and smites down,*
> *And hollow booms the hillside at its fall,*
> *Then do you lead me safely to some cave,*
> *And show me my own self; and in my breast*
> *Deep mysteries and wonders blossom forth.*
> *Then when before my gaze the pure moon rises*
> *Upon her tranquillizing way, there floats*
> *Before me from the rock-walls, and the bushes*
> *Rain-drenched, the ancient world in silver shapes*
> *To soften contemplation's stern delight.*

Gretchen's story closes in this first part of *Faust* as it did in the *Urfaust*, but Mephistopheles' words: 'She is judged' are answered now by choirs of angels saying: 'She is saved.'

XVII. Goethe, Napoleon and France

Goethe suffered, as all other Germans, through the Napoleonic wars and the French occupation, but this did not diminish his admiration for the 'prodigy,' the great man with his unique, 'demonic' power. On the 2nd of October 1808 he was received by the Emperor at Erfurt. He always preserved a certain discretion about this interview, and did not record it in detail until 1824.

The Emperor is seated at a large round table, eating his breakfast. On his right, at some distance from the table, stands Talleyrand, on his left, and fairly near him, Daru, with whom he is discussing something about contributions.

The Emperor signs to me to come forward.

I remain standing at a suitable distance.

After looking at me attentively, he said: 'Vous êtes un homme.'
I bow.

He asks: 'How old are you?'

'Sixty.'

'You are well preserved—'

'You have written tragedies.'

I made the minimum reply.

At this point Daru began to speak.

He spoke of me as my patrons in Berlin are likely to have spoken; I certainly recognized their general attitude and ideas.

He added that I had also made translations from the French, including Voltaire's Mahomet.

The Emperor replied: 'That is not a good play', and gave a detailed analysis of how unsuitable it was that the conqueror of the world should present himself in so unfavorable a manner.

He then turned the conversation to the subject of Werther, *which he appeared to have studied with great thoroughness. After various perfectly just observations, he indicated one particular passage and said: 'Why did you do that? It does not accord with nature,' a point which he went on to discuss at length and with perfect justice.*

I listened with a cheerful countenance, and replied with a gratified smile that I did not know whether anyone else had reproached me with the same thing, but that I thought he was quite right and that I admitted that the passage in question could be shown to be lacking in truth. But, I added, a writer might perhaps be forgiven for making use of a not very obvious artifice in order to bring about certain results which he could not achieve by any simple, natural means.

The Emperor appeared satisfied, and returned to the subject of the drama; he made very penetrating remarks about it, like one who had observed the tragic theatre with all the attention of a criminal judge, and moreover felt deeply about the way French drama had declined from nature and truth.

Thus he spoke with disapproval of the drama of fate, saying that it belonged to a darker age. What do people want with fate nowadays, he said? Politics are fate.

He then turned to Daru again and spoke about the great contribution business. I fell back a little, and took up my stand in that very bay-window where I had, in the past thirty years, spent so many happy and also so many sorrowful hours...

Talleyrand, who had been present during the interview, had gone. Marshal Soult came in. While he conversed with the Emperor, Goethe called to mind his own past experiences in this house.

The Emperor rose, came towards me, and by a sort of manoeuvre cut me out from amongst the others standing beside me.

He turned his back on them and spoke quietly to me, asking whether I was married, and had any children, and other personal matters of common interest. Also about my relations with the ducal family, about the Duchess Amalia, the prince and princess, and so on; I answered him in a natural way. He seemed satisfied, and translated it into his own language, but in a more definite style of expression than I could have permitted myself.

As a general observation, I should add that throughout our conversation I could not but admire the variety of his ways of expressing approval; he seldom listened unmoved, but either nodded his head thoughtfully or said: 'Oui,' or: 'C'est bien' or something of the sort; nor should I forget to remark that when he had spoken himself he usually added: 'Qu'en dit M. Göt?'

Chancellor von Müller's account of the episode and Talleyrand's memoirs contribute a few additional details but add nothing essential.

During the wars of 1813 Goethe held aloof from public life. *The Awakening of Epimenides*, written to order to celebrate the homecoming of the Prussian troops, is an allegorical drama barely recognizable as his. Finding himself accused by his fellow-countrymen of a lack of patriotism, he said one day to Eckermann:

To write war-songs sitting in my own room—a congenial occupation indeed! To do it in a night encampment when you can hear the whinneying of the horses in the enemy's outposts, well and good! But that was not my life nor my work but Theodor Körner's. His war-songs suit him perfectly. But for me, not being of a warlike nature or a warrior's mind, war-songs would have been a mere mask which would have become me very ill.

I have never practised affectation in poetry. What I have not experienced, what has not stung me and driven me to work, to that I have never given poetic expression. I have written love poems only when I was in love. How could I have written songs of hate without hatred? And, between ourselves, I did not hate the French, much as I thanked God when we were quit of them. How could I, for whom the only things that matter are civilization and barbarism, hate a nation which is among the most civilized in the world, and to which I owe so large a part of my own culture?

Generally speaking, national hatred is a peculiar thing. You will always find it strongest and most violent at the lowest levels of culture, but at a certain level it disappears altogether; you are, so to speak, set above nationality, and you feel any joy or suffering of a neighboring people as if it had befallen your own. It is to this level of culture that I belong by nature, and I had established myself in it long before I was sixty. (14th of March, 1830.)

XVIII. **Pandora:** *November 1807 to June 1808*

At the same time as he was finishing the first part of *Faust*, Goethe was thinking about another play. He was filled with sorrow over the war and the defeat and invasion of Germany. His health was often unsatisfactory. He went on working, but without delight. His friends of an earlier period, Lavater and Herder, had died a few years before Schiller. The Duchess Amalia followed in 1807, and his own mother in 1808. There was no fulfilment for his heart in his affection for Christiane; his marriage to her in 1806 was chiefly a grateful recognition of the courage with which she had faced and dealt with the drunken threats of a party of French soldiers. During November 1807 he paid a number of visits to the house of Frommann, a publisher in Jena, and lost his heart to his eighteen-year-old adopted daughter, Minna Herzlieb. But he realized the foolishness of his feelings, and began to absent himself from the house, without letting the Frommanns know why. He now cast his mind back to the hero of his youth, Prometheus, and made him one of the characters in his new work.

His vision had undergone a change. He no longer saw Prometheus primarily as the rebel Titan, but rather as the master of men of action: shepherds, smiths, husbandmen and soldiers. His brother Epimetheus is contrasted with him as the representative of the contemplative life. When Pandora came down to earth Prometheus repulsed her and she was married to Epimetheus. After a while she departed again, leaving Epimetheus their daughter Epimeleia and taking with her their other daughter Elpore.

Epimetheus thinks continually of his past happiness. He feels very much alone in a world where it is the strong men, the men of action, who are the rulers. Elpore appears to him in a dream, and promises to him that Pandora will return.

Epimeleia and Phileros, the son of Prometheus, are in love with one another. Phileros, who, like his father, is a violent man, believes that his love has betrayed him and strikes her with an axe; then, in his desperation, he tries to kill himself. Neither, in fact dies but by their acceptance of sacrifice they have saved the world. Pandora can now return, which means the beginning of a new era of wisdom.

The fragment breaks off at this point. It appears from Goethe's notes that Pandora was to bring to men the revelation of the True and the Beautiful.

In the following lines Epimeleia gives expression to the melancholy of Goethe as he began to grow old:

> One and undisordered, fellow-wanderers,
> Down upon us shine the stars for ever;
> Moonlight silvers over every hilltop,
> And the gusts of wind stir in the foliage,
> And amid the gusts breathes Philomela;
> Gladly with her breathes the youthful bosom
> Wakened from its gracious dream of springtime.
> Why alas, you gods, are all things endless,
> All things; only joy of ours has ending!
>
> Starlight, moon's o'ershimmering, depth of shadow,
> Waterfall and rustling wind, all these are
> Endless; only joy of ours has ending.
>
> Sweetly, hark! a double-lip of grass-blade,
> Sharp and fine, the shepherd boy has fashioned;
> Early through the meadows wide he's sending
> Merry preludes to the noonday crickets.
> But the many-chorded lyre is sounding
> Notes with greater power to hold the heart, and,
> Listening: Who goes wandering there so early?
> Who is singing golden chords without there?
> Maiden longs to know, and sets the shutter
> Soft ajar, and by the shutter listens.
> And the lad can see: there's something moving!
> Who? He longs to know, and lurks and spies there;
> Thus the two are spying on each other,
> Seeing each the other in the half-light.
> And to let what's seen be known more clearly
> And to make what's known a close possession
> Is at once the heart's desire, and arms are
> Oustretched, arms are clasped, a holy union—
> So the heart rejoices in it—sealed thus.
> Why, alas, you gods, are all things endless,
> All things; only joy of ours has ending!
> Starlight and a loving protestation,
> Shimmering moon and tenderest confiding,
> Depth of shade and true love's yearning, these are
> Endless; only joy of ours has ending.

147

XIX. The Elective Affinities*: *1808-1809*

The sources of this novel lie partly in a scientific theory—a chemical law, rather—and partly in Goethe's affection for Minna Herzlieb. He transposed her image into that of Ottilie, a name going back to his early days in Alsace.

'*If you don't think it will seem pedantic,' replied the Captain, 'I can quite well sum it up briefly with conventional signs. Suppose that there is A, intimately bound up with B, and inseparable from it by any number of techniques and any amount of force. Then suppose there is C, similarly related to D. Now bring these two pairs into contact with each other: A will rush to D, and C to B, and it won't be possible to say which first quitted its pair or which first achieved union with the other.*'

Eduard and Charlotte have been married rather late in life, more out of fidelity to an early engagement than out of love. Their friend the Captain is paying them a visit at the time when Charlotte brings her niece to the house. At once the mysterious affinities come into play. The Captain and Charlotte are attracted to each other, while passion impels Eduard towards Ottilie. The latter, an intuitive soul, returns his feeling almost without realizing it, obeying only her own heart.

Charlotte and the Captain bravely renounce one another. The Captain goes away. Charlotte exhorts her husbands to similar conquest of his love. He leaves. During his absence Charlotte gives birth to the child which she conceived by him at the time when the mind of each was full of the image of another. The child,

---

* Sometimes translated as *Kindred by Choice*.

thus conceived in a double moral adultery, bears the features of the Captain and of Ottilie. The latter becomes attached to him and spends much of her time with him.

Eduard returns, finds her and declares his love for her. He has decided to divorce his wife and marry her. She consents. He embraces her, and they have a momentary illusion that it will be possible for them to belong to each other.

In order to return to the house, Ottilie has to cross the lake in a boat, alone except for the child. In the turmoil which she is in she cannot control her movements, and the child is drowned. Grief restores her to herself. She realizes that by consenting to marry Eduard she has violated, in thought, not only the human law of marriage but the law of her own nature. She determines to make expiation. She decides to leave her friends. Eduard finds her and brings her back to the house. She consents, but henceforth she imposes silence on herself as though under a religious vow, and eats only what is strictly necessary to maintain life. She happens one day by chance to hear a friend speaking of the respect needed in marriage. Her emotions are too strong for her. Interiorly worn out, she dies. Eduard, in despair, tries to go on living, as he promised her, but he too dies. Charlotte has them buried side by side.

Such is the main outline of the novel. In construction and language it is wholly classical. It is rich in episodes, and it poses many problems. Goethe repeated to Eckermann the words of a clergyman in Dresden who had expressed astonishment that he, whose ideas on other subjects were so mild, should have such strict principles in regard to marriage. Eckermann added that he found Goethe's remark interesting, since it revealed quite clearly what his true intention had been in writing this novel, wrongly interpreted as it so often was.

The Elective Affinities is primarily a drama of renunciation. Goethe also told Eckermann that he did not care for the personality of Eduard, in whom self-will takes the place of true character, but that he had had to present him in this way in order to carry out his plan. We may note that, of the four characters, Eduard is the only one who makes no renunciation.

At about this same period, Goethe began to revise *Dichtung und Wahrheit*. This is the place to quote the passage later inserted into the sixth book of the memoirs, which was published only after his death but contains much that was written about 1812-13. It expresses the philosophy which, despite one or two passing crises, henceforth guided his life and work.

Both our physical and social life, our morals, customs, worldly wisdom, philosophy and religion, and even many chance happenings as well, all declare to us that we must practice renunciation. *There is so much within us which is so intimately our own and to which we must not give external realization; what we need from outside ourselves for the fulfilment of our being is denied to us, while on the other hand so much of what is thrust upon us is alien and burdensome. We are robbed alike of what we have won by toil and of what we have been gladly accorded in friendship, and before we have clearly realized it we find we are being compelled to give up our personality, first bit by bit and then whole and entire. Add to all this that no one is accorded respect if he rebels under it; on the contrary, the more bitter the cup, the sweeter must be his demeanor, lest some placid onlooker be offended by his grimaces.*

So that he shall be able to accomplish this task, nature has provided man with abundant strength, energy and tenacity. But he is helped especially by that indestructible levity with which he is endowed. This enables him to renounce particular objects moment by moment, so long as in the next moment he can reach out to something fresh; it is thus that we constantly, unconsciously, make good the damage to our lives. We replace one passion with another; occupations, inclination, love affairs, hobbies—we make trial of them all, only to exclaim at last that all is vanity. *No one is horrified at this false and even blasphemous judgment; it is rather supposed to represent something wise and incontrovertible. It is only a few who, with a presentiment of that intolerable feeling, avoid all partial resignations by resigning themselves totally once for all.*

They arrive at a conviction of what belongs to eternal, necessary order, and seek to form such concepts as are imperishable and, so far from being invalidated by the contemplation of transitory things, are rather reaffirmed by it. But because there is in truth something superhuman in all this, such persons are generally considered inhuman, godless and alien to the world; indeed, the one difficulty is to know what precisely in the way of horns and hooves to attribute to them.

Goethe seems here to be stretching out one hand to Pascal and the other to Schopenhauer, while primarily, as is unquestionably the case, making a withdrawal into himself. Because he practiced renunciation, resigned himself, and strove to maintain himself at his own level of wisdom, he too was credited with various 'horns and hooves': impassivity, indifference, and egoism.

XX. **The West-Eastern Divan:** *1814-1816*

In the summer of 1814, with peace restored, Goethe went to spend some time in the Rhineland. He renewed his acquaintance with Willemer, a banker in Frankfurt. The latter had, in the year 1800, taken into his house a young actress, Marianne Jung, in order to remove her from the moral dangers of a theatrical career. He brought her up with his own daughters. Gay, capricious, fanciful, with a graceful wilfulness, she brought all who knew her under her seductive sway. She was thirty when Goethe met her. They were drawn together by a deep feeling of sympathy which appeared so dangerous in Willemer's eyes, despite Goethe's age, that he hastily married Marianne during his friend's absence.

In 1815 Goethe paid another visit to the land of his birth. He spent six weeks with the Willemers. Here, against the old background of his love for Lili, youthful ardor was reawakened in him. But it was only a short while since he had condemned adultery in *The Elective Affinities:* was he to be forever playing Werther? When he felt the bond between this young woman and himself growing too strong, he fled from Marianne as he had twice before fled from Lotte and from Lili. He never saw her again, but to the end of his life he kept up an affectionate correspondence with the Willemers.

This mutual and renunciatory love was the genesis of *The West-Eastern Divan.* For some time Goethe had been interested in the

Marianne von Willemer.

East. His thoughts had taken refuge there during the troubled times of the war and the French occupation. In 1814 he read the two-volume translation of the Persian poet Hâfiz. He began to write poems which at first had no other link with each other than an oriental atmosphere. Soon his love for Marianne gave them a common theme and made them vibrate with a warmer life. He called her Suleika and himself Hatem. And Suleika replied in verses which matched his own genius sufficiently to be worthy of being inserted anonymously amongst his own.

But the *Divan* is not only a love-poem; its inspiration is religious and mystical.

> *To God belongs the Orient!*
> *To God belongs the Occident!*
> *The northern and the southern lands*
> *Rest in peace within His hands.*

Through love, God has expressed Himself in creation. The multiple and scattered creatures which have issued forth from Him retain a nostalgia for that primal Unity into which they yearn to be absorbed once more. In this double movement of diastole and systole, of expansion and concentration, lies the whole drama of the soul. By the sacrifice of its own ego, liberating it from itself, the soul suppresses individuality in order to be consumed in love. This is the thought of Plato, Plotinus and Eckhart; it is also the meaning of Sufic mysticism, whose close relationship with Greek mysticism Goethe discovered. The famous 'Die and come to be!' in the poem 'Blessed Yearning' is more than a striking formulation of Goethe's conviction that evolution is the law of life, as he had shown, for instance, in the 'Metamorphosis of Plants' and the 'Metamorphosis of Animals.' It strikes more deeply into the mystery of being, proclaiming the close relationship between love and death.

> *To wise men tell it, to no others,*
> *For the crowd is quick to mockery:*
> *I would praise that living creature*
> *Which for fiery death has longings.*

> *In the coolness of thy love-nights*
> *Where, engendered, thou engenderest,*
> *Alien feeling comes upon thee*
> *When the silent taper glimmers.*

153

No more dost thou rest imprisoned
In the shadowing of the darkness,
Thou art rapt now by new longing
Upward to a higher espousal.

Distance cannot make thee weary,
Flying, enchanted, thou dost come,
And at last, of light desirous,
Thou art burnt, thou little moth.

Till the day thou make it thine,
This: Die and come to be!
Thou art but a sorrowing guest
In darkness on the earth.

For Hâfiz, as for that Christian mysticism which was born of the Song of Songs, the union of physical love is a symbol of the union of the soul with God. The desire which sweeps Hatem towards Suleika is a figure of the rhythm of the worlds in their subjection to the play of gravitation and affinity, and a figure of the soul irresistibly drawn to God.

Can this be? O star of stars,
I press thee to my heart again!
Ah, the night of separation,
Its abysses and its pain!
Yes, 'tis thou, the sweet, beloved
Counterpart of all my bliss;
I, remembering former sorrows,
Shudder, fearing what now is.

When the world lay deepest buried
There in God's eternal breast
He ordained its hours' beginning
With sublime creative zest,
Spoke the word: Now let it be!
Then rang out an anguished cry
As with mighty strokes the cosmos
Broke into reality.

Light sprang forth: and straight then parted
Darkness from him fearfully,
And at once the elements were
Sundered, each from each must flee.

Swift, in wild unruly dreaming,
All things ever outward pressed,
Straining towards unmeasured spaces,
Longing-less and music-less.

Dumb were all things, waste and silent,
God alone, as ne'er till then!
So the rosy dawn He fashioned
To take pity on the pain;
She from out the gloom drew forth
A singing scale where colors play,
Once again those things could love
Which each from each had fallen away.

And with haste and eager striving
Each seeks each that's truly his;
Towards unmeasured life are turned
Feeling senses, seeing eyes.
Though it be by rape or violence,
Each to each must clasp and hold!
Allah need create no longer,
We it is create His world.

Thus on wings of rosy dawning
I was flung upon thy mouth,
And the night with seals a thousand
Starry-bright confirmed our troth.
We two on this earth a pattern
Set for all, in joy and pain,
Nor could 'Let there be!', though spoken
Once again, part us again.

XXI. *The Last Love and the* **Marienbader Elegie:** *1823*

Some years earlier, a transformation had taken place in Goethe's house. Christiane died in 1816. Goethe's only remaining attachment to her lay in the bonds of habit, but it was a habit which had lasted now for nearly thirty years. In 1817 his son married Ottilie von Pogwisch, and the great house was forthwith filled with grace, animation and disorder. Her faults were as abundant as her qualities: she was intelligent and cultivated, and also a restless, capricious coquette. Her noisy quarreling with August rang in Goethe's ears, but he was very indulgent towards her. She was an accomplished hostess to the endless invited and uninvited guests who came from all over the world to pay homage to the old man. Above all, she gave him three grandchildren: Walther in 1818, Wolfgang in 1820, Alma in 1827.

It was now not unusual for Goethe to be ill. In 1822 he underwent a serious crisis whose nature his doctors did not understand; but, though he came near to death, he recovered so completely that he decided to take his annual cure at Marienbad. He had been attracted there by a young girl, Ulrike von Levetzow. It began as a paternal affection, but quickly changed; now, in 1823, his extraordinary resurgence of youth expressed itself in a renewed desire to love. The atmosphere was fashionable, wordly, laden with sentimental intrigue, against a background of walking parties, music, dinners and *thés dansants*.

His passion for Ulrike now broke out so plainly that Metternich's spies reported it to their master. He was seventy-four; she was nineteen; no more than a sweet, insignificant girl, but for this aura of poetry which now descended upon her. Goethe's thoughts turned to marriage. There are allusions to this intention in his letters to his daughter-in-law which show that he was full of hope. He certainly pondered the drawbacks attendant upon such a marriage: his family's displeasure, and the mockery of the world, for he was one of the most prominent men in Europe, 'the sage of Weimar,' 'the great Goethe.' But his feelings overcame these obstacles; through the duke, he asked for Ulrike's hand.

Whether it was Ulrike herself or her mother who shrank from this improbable union we do not know: the evidence is contradictory. In any case, a reply was given which, if not a refusal, was at least evasive. Once more he was, simply and humanly, un-

157

happy. Those laws of nature to which he gave divine reverence were now crushing him with an inexorable weight; it was decreed that what was still the heart of Werther should now be beating within the shell of an old man. He was not the last to observe the admixture of irony in the sorrowful and pitying smile of fate.

An old man in love is a classic theme of comedy and target for public mockery. But it is not only because Goethe transcends the common measure that ridicule cannot touch him here. Though in him as in any normal being love was accompanied by desire, it was never dominated by it. His love neither for Lotte, nor for Lili, nor, for five years, for Frau von Stein, nor for Suleika—which were the most imperious of his passions—involved physical possession. Except for his poems to Charlotte von Stein as 'Lida' and for the Christiane cycle, his lyrics express the manifold nuances of feeling without erotic allusion. Sometimes, indeed, love rises to the purity of religious feeling: more especially in the *Marienbader Elegie*, in which expressed grief reveals an undercurrent of renunciation, to which the poet has already given consent in his sufferings, though flesh and blood still lag behind. Each of his passions tore at Goethe as though it were the only and the final one, but in another part of his being he always sensed the cure that the future would bring. His farewell to Ulrike overwhelmed him all the more in that he, the great lover, now knew that he was bidding a final farewell to love.

In the carriage which took him back to Weimar he was secretly writing the *Elegie*, while his two companions maintained a respectful silence.

> *What am I now to hope from re-encounter?*
> *From the still folded blossoms of this day?*
> *Both paradise and hell stand open for thee;*
> *What thoughts are in thy mind, there stir and sway!*
> *No more of doubt! To heaven's door she comes,*
> *And thou art lifted high into her arms.*

> *So into paradise thou wast received then,*
> *As worthy that fair, endless life to live;*
> *No longer hadst thou wish or hope or longing,*
> *Here was the goal for which thy heart did strive,*
> *And in the vision of that Only Fair*
> *The spring dried up of all nostalgic tears.*

An angel with a flaming sword thrust him out from his paradise:

> *Fixed, sombre, stares thine eye on thy dark road;*
> *It looks behind, and sees the door is closed.*

The lines flow on, with the poet possessed by sorrow and regret. Through the carriage window the outside world has access to him, and makes its way into the poem as it did when he was writing the 'Storm Song' and the 'Journey in the Harz.'

> *Does not the world remain? These walls of rock,*
> *Are they no longer crowned with holy shadows?*
> *Is not the harvest ripening? Green the landscape*
> *Following the river's course through bush and meadow?*
> *Does not that vastness overarch the world,*
> *Teeming with forms of formless, each by turns?*
>
> *How light and sweet, how clear and delicate-woven,*
> *Seraph-like, floats from that grave choir of clouds,*
> *Seeming like her, in aether's blue above thee*
> *A slender shape of shining vapor now;*
> *In the gay dance thou sawest her thus supreme,*
> *Amid all loveliest forms, the loveliest she.*
>
> *But thou canst venture only for a moment*
> *To embrace a shape of air in place of her;*
> *Back to thy heart! Within 'tis better for thee,*
> *As there her ever-changing image stirs;*
> *For one transforms itself in many there,*
> *A thousandfold, more dear and still more dear.*

Memories return, sweet and tormenting, 'written in flaming letters in this true heart.' He comes back, as in the days of Charlotte von Stein, to the theme of the beloved's presence:

> *Unto the peace of God, which here below*
> *More blessed makes—we read it so—than reason,*
> *I will compare the happy peace of love*
> *In presence of the all-beloved being;*
> *Then is the heart at rest, naught can disturb*
> *Its deepest sense, its sense that it is hers.*
> *There where the heart is purest swells a longing*
> *To give that higher, purer Being Unknown*
> *Freely ourselves in thankfulness, thus reading*
> *The riddle of the Ever-nameless One;*
> *This we call piety; I feel a sharer*
> *In those blest heights whene'er I stand before her.*

What she revealed to him was something he had always known, but her nineteen-year-old light-heartedness made him more vividly aware of it: each passing moment must be eagerly lived for itself. She had restored his joy in working and his sense of the divine. But what was all this to him now?

Now am I far away! The present moment—
What now belongs to it? I cannot tell;
It proffers me much good to serve for beauty,
Which, being but burdensome, I but repel.
Unmastered yearning drives me here and there,
No counsel now remains save boundless tears.

And so, gush forth and flow unchecked; but yet
'Twill never serve to quench the fire within!
Even now, its fierce strength at my breast is tearing,
Where death and life are grimly battling.
Sure, there are herbs which body's pain would still;
But spirit lacks the firm-resolvèd will.

The whole world's lost to me, I to myself,
Who was the darling of the gods but late;
They tested me, bestowed Pandora on me,
So rich in gifts, in peril richer yet;
They pressed me towards that blessing-gifted mouth,
They bar me thence, and thrust me down and down.

Some of Goethe's heroes had turned their backs on life, but there was always a wide gulf between him and them. Notes comparable with these are struck in some of his letters, but he had never before given poetic expression to such suffering as this at the very moment when he was feeling it.

As an epigraph to his poem, he had chosen two lines from *Tasso:*

And though man in his pain be dumb, a god
Gave me the gift to tell of what I suffer.

Back in Weimar, he copied the *Elegie* carefully with his own hand onto fine parchment. He placed it within a cover of red morocco, and even to so intimate a confidant as Eckermann he showed it only much later, with great solemnity. He fell seriously ill again, and during his illness he asked his old friend Zelter, the musician, who had come from Berlin to see him, to read it to him over and over again.

It appears in his works followed by his stanzas in homage to

J. P. Eckermann,
Goethe's secretary from 1823 onwards.

Madame Szymanowska, the beautiful Polish pianist in whose playing he had found consolation at Marienbad and at Weimar, and preceded by the lines 'To Werther' which he wrote for the fiftieth anniversary of the novel; the three together bear the title 'A Trilogy of Passion.'

As late as the New Year of 1824 he wrote to Frau von Levetzow expressing the hope that their wishes that year might be in harmony, and that there should be no obstacle to their 'accomplishment.' But the whole of the poem 'To Werther,' finished at the end of March, expresses a sadness whose source is in the inmost recesses of the soul:

I to remain, thou to depart wast chosen;
Thou didst go on—and much thou hast not lost.

He did not return to Marienbad the following summer.

XXII. Romanticism and 'Universal Literature'

The new generation of Romantic writers who were in the ascendant during Goethe's old age harked back beyond his classical period at Weimar to the old *Sturm und Drang* days at Strasbourg. Like Herder, and Goethe in his youth, they held rationalism in horror, made a cult of individuality, and believed in the primacy of feeling; but they were eclectic enough to subscribe to Hellenic canons, and it is significant that the first theorists of the movement, the brothers Schlegel, gave their review the name of *Athenäum*.

The Romantics hailed Goethe as one of their masters—both the tempestuous twenty-year-old Goethe and the man who had slowly ripened into wisdom. They had a particular admiration for *Wilhelm Meister*, for its fluid construction fulfilled the demands they made upon a work of art, holding as they did that the artist's imagination must acknowledge no law outside itself.

Goethe gave their first efforts a sympathetic reception, though he did not accept all their aesthetic and philosophical theories. He took an interest in Schelling because of his affinities with Spinoza, but he was in agreement neither with his absolute Idealism nor with the doctrine of the supremacy of the ego lying at the heart of Fichte's philosophy, which the Romantics had enthusiastically adopted. Having succeeded, after a lifetime of effort, in imposing limits upon himself, he could take no pleasure in seeing

163

Goethe in 1824,
one year after the Marienbader Elegie.
(*Drawing by K. Chr. Vogel von Vogelstein*).

them cultivating what was sometimes a pathological sensibility. And though he enjoyed music he did not, as they did, accord it priority over the plastic arts; moreover he was suspicious of the music to which they gave their preference, for it was of a kind liable to stir up the demons lurking within man.

Goethe is often quoted as having said: 'I call what is healthy classic and what is diseased romantic,' but, like many similar sayings, it is a sentence which needs its context: 'And the Nibelungen is as classical as Homer, for both are healthy and vigorous. Most of the new stuff is not romantic because it is modern but because it is weak, sickly and diseased, and the old is not classical because it is old but because it is strong, fresh, joyous and healthy. If we use these qualities to distinguish the classic from the romantic, we shall soon be clear about it.'

He was, then, here concerned with a convenient method of classification and with judgments of value. Thus, for instance, his opinion of Victor Hugo varied from one work to another. He admired the lyric qualities of *Les Orientales* and *Odes et ballades*, and loathed *Notre-Dame de Paris*.

His sympathy with the German Romantics grew less and less when their enthusiasm for the Middle Ages began to stimulate among them a number of conversions to Catholicism, some sincere and others inspired more by aesthetic considerations than by real faith. Nor did he share their exaggerated patriotism, tuned to an even higher pitch by the Napoleonic wars; but he was at one with them in their cosmopolitan attitude towards literature. They were enthusiastic admirers of Shakespeare, to whom Goethe had kept allegiance throughout his life, and August Wilhelm Schlegel made a masterly translation of his works into German. As for the English, Goethe read Walter Scott, Carlyle and Byron, the latter with something of the tenderness of a father discovering in a prodigal son the exuberance of his own youth.

Goethe was introduced into France through Madame de Staël's *De l'Allemagne*, and found his warmest admirers there in the writers collaborating in *Le Globe*. He, for his part, looked eagerly towards Paris: 'I am seeking to inform myself on the subject of contemporary French literature, and, if I succeed, will give my opinion on it.' (21st of January 1827.) He read, with great interest, Sainte-Beuve, Vigny, Stendhal, Mérimée—one of his favorites—Balzac, and—a choice which seems odd to modern Frenchmen—Béranger, because of his popular character. Though he did not care for re-reading *Faust* in German, he found it refreshing in

Gérard de Nerval's translation. Generally speaking, he was interested in everything which was being produced in Europe, as he had previously developed his passion for Oriental literature. He had a deep appreciation of Manzoni, and the Romantics drew his attention to poets who had till now been outside the field of his thought—Dante and Calderon.

He read in the original those authors whose languages he knew —French, English, Italian, to make no mention of dead languages. But he also appreciated good translations. He himself produced a considerable number of translations, including works of substantial length: *Reineke Fuchs* from Low German (1793-4), *Benvenuto Cellini* from Italian at the time of his friendship with Schiller, Voltaire's *Mahomet* and *Tancrède* (1799-1800), and Diderot's *Le Neveu de Rameau* at a time when it was still in manuscript and as yet unknown in France. He welcomed such exchanges, which were to usher in a new universal literature in which all men of taste and culture would be able to participate.

It is very satisfactory that now, with the close ties that there are between the French, English and Germans, we shall be in a position to correct each other. This is the great advantage which will result from a universal literature, and it will become clearer and clearer as time goes on. (15th of July 1827.)

National literature no longer means very much today; the time has come for universal literature, and we should all be working to hasten its arrival. But in thus valuing what is foreign to us we should not single out anything in particular and try to regard it as a model— neither Chinese literature nor Serbian, neither Calderon nor the Nibelungen; when we need a model, we must constantly go back to the ancient Greeks, whose works always represent the beauty of man. Everything else we must consider only historically, and appropriate the good that is in it as far as it goes. (31st of January 1827.)

I owe much both to the Greeks and to the French; my debt to Sterne and Goldsmith is infinite. But these are not enough to indicate the sources of my culture; for that there would be no stopping, nor is it necessary to do it. The essential thing is to have a soul which loves truth and welcomes it wherever it finds it. (16th of December 1828.)

Warum stehen sie davor?
Sind nicht Thüre da und Thor?
Kämen sie getrost herein
Würden wohl empfangen seyn.
Goethe 1828

*Goethe's house at Weimar,
from a drawing by Otto Wagner (1827).*

XXIII. Wilhelm Meister's Years of Wandering

The *Years of Wandering*, in production from 1798 onwards, was revised several times over before the final version of 1829. Anyone approaching it with the hope of encountering once more the rich vein of the *Years of Apprenticeship*—especially the original *Theatrical Vocation*—with its wealth of episodes and its host of characters teeming round the hero can only look for disappointment. The sequel is still, indeed, a novel, but according to a quite different formula. It is slow-moving, with interruptions in the form of more or less independent short stories, long dissertations and aphorisms. The characters have none of the solidity of their predecessors. But if, on the other hand, we look for what Goethe really meant to put into it, we shall admire its rich quality. His genius was soon to pronounce its final message in the form of *Faust*. The *Years of Wandering* are a preliminary statement of that conclusion. Wilhelm Meister is no aged Titan; yet, at the very height of his maturity he imposes limitations upon himself. *Wilhelm Meister's Years of Wandering, or Renunciation.* It is a long, elaborately presented pedagogical thesis, the summit of the old sage's doctrine.

To cure Wilhelm of his instability, the Company of the Tower takes him away from Nathalie and sets him the task of continual travel. He is not to sleep more than three nights under the same roof, nor to return within a year to any place which he has left. He sets out with his son Felix.

At the heart of the book lies the 'Province of Pedagogues,' to which Wilhelm is shortly to entrust his son. This is one of the most famous passages in the book. The Three by whom Wilhelm is received explain to him their method of education.

To each person, nature has given all that he needs for the present and the future. Our duty is to develop it: often it develops best of itself. But there is one thing which no one brings with him into the world, and yet it is upon it that everything depends, if a man is to be in every respect a man. If you can discover it for yourself, name it. Wilhelm thought for a brief moment and then shook his head.

After a suitable pause they cried 'Reverence!'

The three degrees of reverence find their expression in the three forms of salutation successively imposed upon the pupil. Reverence for what is above us: for God, and also for parents and superiors who hold their authority from Him; reverence for what is below us: for the earth and the terrestrial elements; reverence for companions and equals, 'for only in union with his fellows can he confront the world.'

In the Province, religion is held in esteem only when it is inspired by reverence, not by fear. Ethnic religion reveres what is above us: such is pagan religion once it is released from fear. Then comes philosophical religion, based on reverence of equals, of the wise man for his fellows. The Christian religion is based upon reverence for that which is below us. 'This is the final point to which humanity could and must attain... to recognize as divine, abasement and poverty, derision and scorn, shame and misery, suffering and death; more, to venerate and hold dear even sin and crime, as being not obstacles but helps to holiness!... Once it has reached this point humanity cannot withdraw from it, and we may say that the Christian religion... once having appeared, cannot disappear; once having become divinely incarnate, can never again be dissolved.'

Of these three degrees of reverence is born the supreme reverence, reverence for oneself.

The Province does not abandon each pupil to his own bent. Its principles resemble Nathalie's: 'Nothing is to be left to the caprice of the pupil.' He has to obey 'severe demands and strict laws.' The pupils study music, the living languages, and the plastic arts or architecture. Dramatic art is strictly forbidden. At the same time as their minds and souls are developed, they are given physical training exercises and made to cultivate the soil. Felix, who has no aptitude for the latter, turns to the training of horses.

This pattern of the education of children reflects what Goethe recommends for the grown man. One of the leaders of the Company explains to Wilhelm the need for specialization and service:

Make yourself into a specialized organ, and then wait for whatever place humanity is good enough to allot you in the life of the community... It is better to limit oneself to a trade. For lesser minds, it will always be a trade; for better ones, an art; and for the best, in doing one thing he does all, or, to put it less paradoxically, in that one thing which he does well he sees the symbol of all that is well done.'

Each must develop his own personal gift to its utmost limits. Friedrich, who has a good memory and fine handwriting, is to become a secretary; the frivolous Philine a dressmaker; Lenardo is to work in wood and metal. As for Wilhelm, his childhood memories and his adventure with the brigands prompt him to choose surgery. Thanks to this decision he is dispensed from having to move continually from place to place.

In his youth Goethe had lived in eighteenth-century society among nobles and bourgeois who were in general more anxious to cultivate their own ego than to work for the common good. Now, individualism of the Werther type had been replaced by a new but almost identical *mal du siècle*, while social upheavals due to the development of the machine and of capitalism were threatening to set owners and proletariat over against each other as opposing forces. Goethe was showing the former how to use their wealth for the good of all, and the latter how to better themselves through culture.

The *Years of Wandering* presents the life of society in many forms: a quasi-patriarchal artisan community; a cotton-spinning mill in the mountains, making use of modern methods; and more advanced enterprises. The Uncle has come from America and remained in Europe out of love for European culture, 'that inexhaustible culture which was born many thousands of years ago, which has grown up, which has been checked and damaged but never completely crushed, and which is beginning to breathe again, to come to life again and to be manifest in innumerable activities.' The Uncle has brought to Europe those social conceptions which dominated the emigrants to America. On the walls of his house are to be read such inscriptions as: 'From the useful to the beautiful through the true. Possessions and goods in common.'

One part of the Company which received Wilhelm into it is to remain in Europe; the other is to leave for America with Lenardo. Goethe put into the mouth of the latter some of the doctrines which he had most at heart: 'Let everyone seek to be useful to himself and to others. Whatever man may undertake and do, an individual is never sufficient unto himself; society is always the supreme need of a man of worth. All useful men ought to be in relationship with each other, as the patron is to the architect, and he to the mason and the carpenter.'

Such is the teaching of the man who is described, precisely at this period of his life, as an egoist and an Olympian.

The members of the Company pledge themselves to honor all religions and accept all forms of government. We see here both the tolerance of Goethe in his old age and his indifference to political questions.

Practical activity, however, does not exclude contemplation. The latter is represented in the Company by the strange figure of Macarie, who is somehow incorporated into the solar system and identified with the soul of the world. In her intuition the exterior and interior worlds are united. She understands and advises, and her active love goes out to all. For her there is no longer any question of obedience to the moral law: it has become the natural bent of her being. She is the crowning figure in a novel which glorifies 'useful' work, and, after Ottilie in *The Elective Affinities*, the Beautiful Soul, and Nathalie, she is one of the noblest incarnations of the Eternal Feminine which Goethe has given us.

Goethe in 1828.
(Colored sketch by J. K. Stieler).

XXIV. God and the Soul

A study of Goethe's religious thought reveals it as having been extremely fluid. Within his works can be found statements of it which are extremely divergent, not only those separated by a period of years but those which belong to the same period. Hence anyone can claim agreement with him by reference to some particular quotation, and many have permitted themselves to do so. He himself deliberately opened the door to these contradictory interpretations when he wrote to Jacobi, on the 6th of January 1813: 'Being by nature of so many various tendencies, I cannot satisfy myself with one way of thinking. As a poet and artist I am a polytheist, but as a natural scientist I am a pantheist—and as convincedly one as the other. If for my personal life, as a moral being, I have need of a God, that too is taken care of.' To Jacobi too he described himself as 'an old pagan,' and 'the last of the pagans.'

One source of such contradictions is that Goethe was often ready to adapt himself to the language of his correspondent. Unless, on the contrary, he reacted with irritation against an attempt at proselytizing. He did so in his youth with Lavater. When his former friend Auguste von Stolberg, now Countess Bernstorff, wrote to him after many years of silence to admonish him to seek 'Him who loves so much to let Himself be found by men,' the first part of his reply, written on the 17th of April 1823, consists in

171

taking refuge in solemn platitudes. He goes on in a rather more personal, deferential, friendly tone, faintly tinged with condescension, but continues to be reticent:

All my life I have aimed at honesty towards myself and others, and in the midst of all earthly business I have always raised my eyes to that which is highest; and so have you and yours. Then let us go on working so long as it is still day for us; for others too a sun will shine, and they will blossom out in it and so shed a brighter light upon us.

So let us be untroubled about the future! In our Father's kingdom there are so many provinces, and since He has prepared so happy a dwelling for us here below, surely provision will be made for both of us, too, up there. Perhaps we shall attain then to what has eluded us so far—to get to know each other face to face, and so to love each other more deeply. Keep your memories of me faithfully and tranquilly.

He broke off the letter when he became seriously ill, and added, in a postscript, that 'the Ruler of All has granted me still to behold the lovely light of His sun; may day look no less graciously upon you... May everything meet at last once more in the arms of the all-loving Father.'

With some simplification, we may say that Goethe was in his youth attached to a form of Christianity pietistic in tendency and somewhat tinged with pantheism; in the period of which the Italian journey was the climax he was resolutely 'pagan,' clinging to this world and to no other values than those of ancient paganism; and that in the last phase of his life his inclination was once more towards mysticism, to which the *Divan* already bears witness: 'To each age of man corresponds a particular philosophy... An old man will always make confession of mysticism... Old age finds peace in Him who is, who was and who will be.'

But needless to say we shall never, at any period, find an affirmation of any one of these tendencies except with all the others underlying it.

If Goethe drew nearer again to Christianity in his old age, it was a Christianity without dogmas. Thus, he bluntly repudiated the doctrine of the Trinity:

I believed in God, in nature, and in the victory of good over evil, but this was not enough for the pious souls, I had to believe as well that three is one and one is three; but that conflicted with the sense of truth in my soul; nor did I see how it could be of the slightest help to me. (To Eckermann, 4th of January 1824.)

Christ still inspired in him the same respect as always. 'Every

172

act and word of Christ gives testimony of a higher reality. Starting from commonplace things. He always ascends to the heights, drawing others after him.' But he did not recognize Him as divine in the Christian sense: 'Jesus, pure in feeling, thought in silence of one God alone; they who make of him a God offend against his holy will.' (From the *Divan*, posthumous poems.)

Goethe remained as deeply attached to the Bible as in his youth, a point on which he scarcely changed at all. In regard to its authenticity, he said to Eckermann, on the 11th of March 1832, the very month of his death:

I regard all four gospels as wholly authentic, for there is at work in them the reflection of a sublimity, emanating from the person of Christ, which is as divine in character as anything of a divine nature which has ever yet appeared upon earth. If anyone asks me whether it is in my nature to offer him adoring reverence, I answer: Entirely so! I bow down before him as before the divine manifestation of the highest principle of morality. If anyone asks me whether it is in my nature to venerate the sun, I answer again: Entirely so! For it too is a manifestation of the Highest, and indeed the mightiest manifestation of which it is granted to us sons of earth to be aware. In it I adore the light and the generative power of God, through which alone we live and move and are, and all the plants and animals with us. But if anyone asks me whether I feel inclined to bow down before a thumb-bone of the Apostle Peter or Paul, then I answer: Spare me, and take your absurdities elsewhere!

We can sense here a resurgence of his earlier revulsion against the wholly external Catholicism by which he had several times been shocked during his stay in Italy. He seems too to have expressed on this occasion a greater degree of sympathy towards Protestantism than he had felt in his youth:

We simply do not know what we have to thank Luther for, and the Reformation in general. We have been freed from the chains of intellectual restriction; because of our cultural progress we have been able to go back to the source and grasp Christianity in its purity... However much intellectual culture progresses, however much the natural sciences develop in width and depth, however much the human mind grows in breadth, it will never go beyond the sublimity and moral culture of Christianity, as it shines and radiates in the Gospels! But the more courageously we Protestants press forward in this noble evolution, the more swiftly will the Catholics follow. As soon as they feel themselves caught up in the great and ever more embracing enlightenment of this age, they will have to follow, whatever they may

173

try to do about it; and so it will come about that at last all will be one.

Thus Goethe in his old age inclined towards a religious universalism imbued with a deep respect for the sacred.

People use the divine name as though the Supreme Being, the incomprehensible, of whom it is impossible to form any idea whatever, were nothing much more than themselves... If they were filled with a sense of His greatness they would be silent and would, through veneration, avoid naming Him. (To Soret, 31st of December 1823.)

The only idea which we can have of that greatness is through nature, in which He has partly revealed Himself. But He is more than a purely immanent God, more personal than God-Nature:

I do not enquire whether this supreme being possesses intelligence and reason; I feel that He is intelligence and reason itself. All creatures are penetrated with it, and man has so much of it that he can recognize parts of the Most High. (To Eckermann, 23rd of February 1831.)

And must not Love be one of His primary names? One day Eckermann told him a story of two wrens which were given shelter and food in a robin's nest. 'The man who can hear that and not believe in God is past the help of Moses and the prophets,' said Goethe. 'That is what I call the omnipresence of God, who has disseminated and planted everywhere a fragment of His infinite love, showing already in bud in an animal that which comes to its fairest flower in a good man.' (8th of October 1827.)

What of the soul, and personal survival? Though not presented in systematic form, Goethe's final philosophy is an attempt at a compromise between the thought of Spinoza and that of Leibniz. He supposes that Spinoza's substance contains certain 'primary elements,' spiritual forces which are unchangeable in their essence but capable, through personal effort, of corresponding more or less fully with that idea which they bear within themselves. Goethe sometimes uses the vocabulary of Leibniz, and calls them monads, and sometimes that of Aristotle, giving them the name of entelechies; God is the supreme entelechy.

He discussed this problem with Falk, in a famous conversation which took place on the day of Wieland's funeral, 25th of January 1813.

In the matter of our soul's personal survival after death, this is how I look at things. It in no way contradicts the observations which I have been making for many years of our nature and that of all natural beings; on the contrary, it emerges from those observations with fresh persuasive force. But how much or how little of this per-

sonality deserves to survive is another question, and a point which we must leave to God...

Concerning the fate of the 'primary elements': 'All the monads are so indestructible that at the moment of dissolution they do not come to an end or lose their activity, but continue it in that same moment. Thus they leave their former condition only to enter instantly upon a new condition.'

But there is a hierarchy amongst them. It is only the higher monads which have a personal survival and participate in the joy of creative energy. Judging by the end of the Helena act in the second part of *Faust*, Goethe regarded the others as destined to return to elemental life: 'I do not doubt our permanent duration,' he said, again, to Eckermann, on the 1st of September 1829, 'for nature cannot do without the entelechy; but we are not all immortal in the same way, and if anyone is to be manifested in the future as a great entelechy, he must first of all be one.'

Throughout his life he based his theories on experience, and he said once more to Falk that he was not in the habit 'of recognizing any exclusive value in ideas which have no basis in anything which can be represented to the senses. But at the point where experimental science stops, another realm begins: let us not demonstrate what simply cannot be demonstrated... Where science is sufficient, we have, it is true, no need of faith, but where science loses its force or shows itself inadequate we must not dispute the rights of faith.'

Let us continue to work, [he wrote to Zelter on the 19th of March 1827] *until, first one and then the other, we are summoned by the World Spirit to return to the aether. May that eternally living Being not deny to us then the exercise of new faculties analogous to those in which we have already given proof of ourselves! If He then, in His fatherliness, grants us a memory and after-taste of whatever we have already willed or achieved that is right and good, then surely we shall be all the quicker in taking hold upon the interacting workings of the world. A monad-entelechy has nothing to do but continue in tireless activity. If it succeeds in making this a second nature, then it will never lack occupation through all eternity.'

Goethe in his study, dictating to his secretary John.
(Painting by J. J. Schmeller).

XXV. The Second Part of Faust

Between 1825 and 1832 Goethe was working at the second part of *Faust*, one of the richest works in world literature: 'incommensurable,' to use his own comment, and containing many difficult passages, but, for sheer density of thought, rivaled only by Dante and Shakespeare; shimmering with poetry and glorious in language.

After the Gretchen tragedy—Faust's failure in the experience of love—we find him gathering strength once more in the bosom of nature.

Then, with Mephistopheles as his companion, he goes to the Emperor's court, which is in a bad way, its finances being in a disastrous condition. Mephistopheles undertakes to provide money. In the anticipation of wealth to come the Emperor takes part in the festivities of the carnival, which give Goethe the opportunity to dazzle the reader with a masque reminiscent of the court festivities of his early days in Weimar and of the spectacle of the Roman Carnival. Faust assumes the allegorical guise of Plutus.

Mephistopheles' remedy for the financial deficit consists of an issue of notes. Everyone is delighted with the abundance resulting from this flood of spurious money. The Emperor, having seen Faust indulging in a series of fantastic tricks in the course of the masque, supposes him to be a magician and demands that he shall conjure up Helen and Paris. Mephistopheles confesses himself powerless in the matter, for Goethe was unwilling to allow him inaugurative control over classical beauty. To find Helen, Faust goes down into the place of the Mothers (the world of Platonic ideas? the realm of monads?). Helen represents at once sensual enjoyment and ideal beauty. Faust tries to grasp her, but she is only an image. After a brief return to his laboratory, where he produces an artificial man, Homunculus—a reminiscence of Goethe's books of alchemy— he continues his search for Helen in the enchanted world of the Classical Walpurgis Night, to which Mephistopheles unwillingly accompanies him. Faust is granted his request for Helen's resurrection by Persephone. Arrayed as a German knight, he wins her love and they are united, a symbol of the union of the Greek with the Germanic genius. They have a son, Euphorion, the incarnation of modern poetry with all its extravagances, of which Byron was, in Goethe's eyes, the type.

Euphorion's existence is short. He believes that he has wings, and he falls to his death, calling to his mother, who follows him into death. She leaves Faust only her robe and her veil:

FAUST: *Yet still there floats a soft and shining wisp of cloud*
      Around my breast and brow, with cheering, cool caress.
      And now it rises, light and wavering, higher on high,
      Takes shape.—Am I deceived in this most lovely form,
      Best good of my first youth, that I have lacked so long?
      My earliest treasures, deepest in my heart, surge up:
      The impulsive lightness and the love of my aurora
      It shows me—that first sight, swift-felt, scarce understood,
      Which, still held fast, has shone upon all treasures since.
      Like spirit's loveliness, that gracious form still grows,
      And, not dissolving, mounts into the air away,
      And with it draws away the best that is in me.

For Faust, it is Margarethe and Helen. For Goethe, it is the image, at once multiple and one, extending from Gretchen to Ulrike.

This episode of Beauty has been an experience rather than a sin on Faust's part. Now he is to undergo the temptation of power. He desires to possess, to dominate. A state of anarchy prevails in the Empire, the reigning Emperor being confronted by an anti-Caesar. With Mephisto's help the Emperor wins, and as a reward Faust obtains his wish: a fief bordered by the sea, where he has scope for action. This brings us to Act V, which Goethe wrote in 1831-32, only a few months before his death.

Faust is, then, in possession of a vast and prosperous province, which he extends by winning further tracts of land from the sea. The carrying out of these great enterprises has required the sacrifice of many human lives.

Surveying all the landscape stands Lynkeus the Watchman. In his song we find the final statement of the old poet's image of himself: for he had been a master of vision, and had given a resolutely affirmative response to destiny, as in another line written in 1828: 'Whatever life may be, it is good.'

Lynkeus the Watchman sings:

> *Born but for seeing,*
> *Set here to behold,*
> *And vowed to my tower*
> *I delight in the world.*
> *I gaze at what's far*
> *And I look at what's near,*
> *The moon and the stars,*
> *The woods and the deer.*
> *In everything seeing*
> *A beauty endless,*
> *Delighting in this*
> *I delight in myself.*
> *O eyes, you are blessed!*
> *Whate'er you have seen,*
> *And however it be, yet*
> *Most fair it has been!*

Faust would be able to feel himself an absolute master if it were not for one old couple, symbolically named Philemon and Baucis, who refuse to give up their humble little property to him: it is a house on the hillside beside a little chapel whose bell maddeningly and continually reminds Faust that that is where his power comes to an end. Mephisto understands Faust's secret desire, and receives his half-explicit authorization: the old people are to be given another property in exchange. But Mephisto burns their cottage and kills them. Then, as after the Gretchen tragedy, Faust is overwhelmed with remorse. He renounces magic. Henceforward he intends to confront nature only as a simple human being.

Four grey-clad women appear to him: Want, Debt, Necessity and Care, the last alone capable of making her way into a rich man's house:

> *In forms that ever vary*
> *I use my cruel power:*
> *Along the pathway, on the wave,*
> *An ever-anxious fellow-traveler,*
> *Always found, never sought,*
> *As often fawned upon as cursed.*
> *Hast thou never known Care?*

FAUST: *I have but run through all the world;*

> *Each thing I wanted seizing by the hair,*
> *Let go what did not satisfy,*
> *And what evaded me, let fly.*
> *I have but craved, and then have but achieved,*
> *And yet again desired, and so with might*
> *Stormed through my life: first mightily and grandly,*
> *But now in wisdom, and reflectively.*
> *This sphere of earth I know now, well enough.*
> *Against our upward vision a bar is set;*
> *Fool, who directs thither his dazzled eyes,*
> *Fancying above the clouds one like himself!*
> *Let him stand fast and look around him here!*
> *To a man of worth and power this world's not dumb.*
> *Why need he haver in eternity?*
> *All that he knows here grasped can be.*
> *Thus let him pass along his earthly day:*
> *Though ghosts may squitter, let him go his way,*
> *In pressing onwards find his pain and bliss,*
> *Each moment still in discontentedness!*

Faust seems, then, to be very far indeed from fulfilling the condition of the pact by bidding the passing moment stay. Care takes little account of his words. She breathes upon his face and takes away his sight: 'Men all the days they live are blind. So be thou, Faust, now at the end!'

Faust's will is unbroken: 'Deep and more deep the night seems pressing in, But yet within there shines a brilliant light.'

He calls his servants to carry out the work which he has conceived, but those who come are hideous lemures obeying the summons of Mephisto. Faust rejoices as the sound of their spades falls on his ear, but in reality they are digging his grave.

FAUST:
> *There lies a swamp along the hills,*
> *Infecting all that we have won;*
> *To drain away that foul stagnation too—*
> *This final conquest were the noblest one!*
> *I open thus this land for many millions*
> *To live, not safely, but in strenuous freedom.*
> *Green lie the fields, and fruitful! Men and cattle*
> *Are soon at home upon the new-made earth,*
> *Set in the shelter of that mighty hill*
> *Raised by a people's bold, unflagging work!*
> *Here lies, within, a paradisical land,*
> *While there, without, the waves roar on the dyke,*

> And as they gnaw it, threatening huge invasion,
> All throng together in haste to close the gaps.
> Yes! Of this mind I am, and wholly am,
> And this is wisdom's final say:
> None can deserve his freedom or his life
> Save he who wins them day by day!
> And so will pass, by danger ringed around,
> The sturdy days of childhood, manhood, age.
> That teeming life could I but see,
> Stand on free land amid a people free!
> Then might I to the moment say:
> 'Stay yet awhile, thou art so fair!
> The imprint of my earthly days
> Shall not for aeons disappear!'
> And in the foretaste of that joy sublime
> Even now I taste that highest point of time.

[He falls. The lemures seize him and lay him on the ground.]

MEPHISTOPHELES: *No pleasure could him sate, nor joy content,*
> *But ever-changing shapes he'd still be wooing;*
> *This final, wretched, empty little moment,*
> *Poor soul, he chooses to clasp to him.*
> *Who was so mighty to withstand*
> *Me, time has conquered: here he lies, an old man,*
> > *[in the sand!*
> *The clock has stopped—*

CHORUS: > > > > *Has stopped, to midnight*
> > > > *[silence stilled*
> *The hand has fallen—*

MEPHISTOPHELES: > > > *Fallen! It is fulfilled.*

CHORUS: *And all is past!*

MEPHISTOPHELES: *Past! That's a stupid word. Why past?*
> *Past and pure nothingness: that's simply all the*
> > *[same!*
> *What use, then, to be endlessly a-doing?*
> *Bearing what's done away to nothingness?*
> *'It's past!' What's to be said of that?*
> *It might as well have never been,*
> *And yet it treads the wheel as though it were!*
> *I'd gladly change that for an endless void.*

But is it possible that Mephistopheles should be the victor?
Even supposing that such a conditional statement ('*Then might I
to the moment say...*') could give him any rights over Faust,

what sort of fulfilment was it which he thus anticipated? His desire was to be of use to others: if we may use a Christian term for it—for it is to this vocabulary that Goethe himself is now about to turn—this great moment has come about in the context not of egotistical pleasure but of charity. Then how could it possibly hand him over to the powers of evil?

So, after a brief struggle with Mephistopheles and his demons, the angels triumph, 'bearing away that which is immortal in Faust'.

Heaven opens. The first to appear are the holy anchorites, against the background of a mountainous landscape. They sing, their chants alternating with those of blessed children. The angels who come bearing the soul of Faust sing an echo to the words spoken by the Lord in the Prologue:

> *A noble piece of spirit-life*
> *Is saved from power of evil:*
>
> '*Whoever strives, and tireless strains,*
> *Him we can still deliver.*'
>
> *Since love itself has from above*
> *Come down to take his part,*
> *The blessed host shall meet him now*
> *With welcome from the heart.*

THE BLESSED CHILDREN: *Gladly receive we*
This soul in his chrysalis;
Whom we accept thus
In promise an angel is.
Loose now the swathings
Round him entwined!
See, he grows beautiful
With holy life.

The Doctor Marianus sings the praises of the Mater Gloriosa who now appears. Then speaks the choir of penitents, whose hands poured forth the shower of roses which helped the angels to win their victory:

CHOIR OF PENITENTS: *Thou soarest to heights*
Of the infinite realms;
Accept thou our prayers,
Thou peerless,
Thou full of grace!

MAGNA PECCATRIX
(St. Lucae XII, 36):

By that love which on the feet
Of thy God-transfigured Son
Let the tears flow down like balm,
Spite of Pharisaic scorn,
By the vessel which so richly
Poured its sweet scent over Him,
By the tresses which so softly
Wiped and dried His holy limbs—

MULIER SAMARITANA
(St. Joh. IV):

By that spring where, long ago,
Abraham would lead his sheep,
By that pail to whose cool touch
Was given to meet the Savior's lip,
By that pure, abundant fountain
Which from thence is gushing now,
Overflowing, ever gleaming,
And through all the worlds doth flow—

MARIA AEGYPTIACA
(Acta Sanctorum):

By that place of all most sacred
Where the Lord was laid to rest,
By the arm which from the doorway,
Warningly, me backward pressed,
By my forty faithful years
Of penance in the desert land,
By the glad salute of parting
Written by me in the sand—

THE THREE:

Thou who to the greatest sinners
Dost thy presence not deny,
And dost lift the prize of penance
High into eternity,
Grant to this dear soul as well,
Who but once herself forgot,
And who knew not she was sinning,
Pardon equal to her lot!

UNA POENITENTIUM, joining herself to them; whose name was
formerly Gretchen:

Bow down, bow down,
Thou peerless one,
Thou rich in radiance,
Thy gracious face upon my joy!
He, first beloved,
No longer troubled,
Comes back to me.
... Ringed by the choir of lofty spirits,
And, in his newness, scarce aware,

> He hardly senses his fresh life,
> Though one with all the holy choir.
> See how he tears the veils away
> Of every former bond of earth,
> How from his airy raiment now
> His first young strength comes freely
> [forth!
>
> O grant it me to be his teacher,
> Still dazzled by the day is he.

MATER GLORIOSA:
> Come, soar thyself to higher spheres!
> Sensing thee, he will follow thee.

CHORUS MYSTICUS:
> All that is transient
> Is but an image;
> What was unperfected
> Here finds fulfilment;
> What is unsayable,
> Here it is done;
> The Eternal Feminine
> Still leads us on.

Since there already exists a vast number of mutually incompatible interpretations of this final scene, it can only be left to speak for itself; but we should not forget that Goethe himself commented upon it to Eckermann: '. . . In Faust himself, an activity which is ever higher and purer to the very end, and eternal love coming down from on high to his aid. This is entirely in harmony with our religious ideas, according to which we are saved not only by our own strength but by divine grace which comes to supplement it.' (6th of June 1831.)

Goethe carefully sealed his work, which was to be given to the world only after his death. It is this, even more than the meaning of the text itself, which is such a mystery. Did he dread comments on his ending as being too 'Catholic'? Symbolism, say almost all the critics. No doubt it is so, but who would ever dare to suggest that Goethe was wholly without sympathy for the Greeks when he borrowed characters and legends from them, or that he was unfriendly to oriental symbolism when he was finding inspiration in Hâfiz? There is no denying that it was these 'Catholic' images, the 'symbolism' of grace obtained for a soul through repentance, penance, and the prayers of other souls, in the name of Christ, which seemed to him the most valid form in which to render his ultimate and supreme thought.

XXVI. The End: March 22nd 1832

Thus Goethe had passed his eightieth year, a center of admiration to the whole world. There was only one intellectual matter on which he felt any bitterness, and this should perhaps be described as a weakness. With few exceptions, the world of professional science did not recognize his scientific work as having the importance which he himself attached to it: 'Of all that I have done as a poet I make no account. There have been excellent poets living in my own time, others, better still, before me, and others again will come after me; but that I should be the only man of my century to know the truth about the difficult science of colors is a matter on which I feel some complacency; hence I do have a sense of being superior to many.' (To Eckermann, 19th of February 1829.)

The legend of the impassible Olympian had begun to establish itself. He knew of it; what did he say of it? 'I have always been regarded as one peculiarly favored by destiny; to be sure, I have no wish to complain nor to curse the course of my life, but, fundamentally, it has been nothing but sorrow and travail.'

Had he then forgotten the good hours? The days at Sesenheim? Lili's smile? His dreams of Italy and their long-delayed fulfilment? His love for Frau von Stein (now a very old lady, long reconciled to him)? He suffered the sad fate of old men who have to see the number of the empty places around them slowly multiplying. Frau von Stein died in 1827, the duke in 1828; his only son, August who had been a source of so little satisfaction to him, died at Rome in 1830.

To the very end of his life, Goethe went on reading and working, and conversing with his associates: his archivist, Riemer, Chancellor von Müller, Coudray, the architect, and Soret, the young prince's tutor. He took an interest in a wide variety of subjects. He also spoke sometimes of his works, and one of the last things he

said about himself is stamped with that humility about his own genius and destiny which marked him all his life:

Fundamentally, we are all collective beings... We all have to receive and to learn, both from those who went before us and from our own contemporaries... I have, it is true, done and achieved various things in my long life of which I might perhaps boast. But if we are to be honest, what had I that was truly my own, except a capacity and inclination for seeing and hearing, for selecting and choosing, and for giving a certain spiritual animation and appropriate form to what I had seen and heard? I certainly do not owe my works to my own wisdom alone, but to thousands of things and people outside myself who gave me the materials for them. (17th of February 1832.)

On the 16th of March Vogel, his doctor, was called at eight o'clock in the morning. Goethe had caught a chill the previous evening, and had passed a bad night. During the two following days he got so much better that he was able to read—in French—and to look at some engravings, but on the night of the 19th-20th he went through a series of violent crises, though he would not allow his servant to give the doctor the trouble of coming. The doctor did not visit him again until the morning of the following day, and was struck by the agitated behavior of the old man, usually so deliberate in all his movements. His pain drove him restlessly from his bed to his chair, his face was ashy grey, and his whole look was of a man in his death agony.

The doctor's ministrations produced a fresh improvement. Goethe listened to his grandson Walther telling him a story. In the evening he sent his daughter-in-law and the children away, and told his servant to lie down on his own bed, while he himself sat in the chair. He slept a little. Early in the morning he took a few steps in his study, but he had to go back at once to his chair.

The doctor had been able to hold out no hope. At about sunrise his condition grew worse. He fell into a half-slumber, asked for a box of drawings which he thought he saw before him, woke up, and realized that it was only a 'phantom.' His thoughts were growing confused, and turned to Schiller: seeing a paper on the floor he said that they must not let his friend's letters lie about like that. He spoke once more: 'Do open the other shutter and let more light into the room.'

When his speech failed, he drew shapes in the air, and then traced a few lines with his right forefinger. When he no longer had strength for this he went on making letters on the coverlet which

187

was laid over his knees. It was possible to make out nothing except a W.

Then he settled comfortably into the left hand side of the chair and breathed his last.

It was on the 22nd of March 1832, at about half past eleven in the morning. Spring had begun.

'More light!' the last words attributed to him, were really spoken. He, indeed, meant no more by them than a request to have the shutters opened. But there is no need to reproach posterity for having given a symbolic sense to these last words of the man who gave to his life's work, *Faust*, the ending: 'All that is transient is but an image.'

Goethe's extremely simple bedroom, opening out of his study, in the great house on the Frauenplan in Weimar. He died in the armchair beside the bed.

SOME OPINIONS

Some Opinions

You cannot ask anyone explicitly: What do you think of heaven and earth? What is your opinion of men and of human life? Are you a reasonable creature or a wretched imbecile? But all these delicate matters are summed up in the trite question: What do you think of Goethe? For, since we all have the works of Goethe set before us, we can rapidly compare the judgment of anyone else upon them with our own; this gives us a fixed scale upon which to measure all his thoughts and feelings, so that he will, unconsciously, have passed judgment upon himself.

HEINRICH HEINE

A man for whom I feel admiration, but no affection whatever.

CHATEAUBRIAND

If, in that atmosphere of glory which you inhabit, an obscure and humble tribute cannot touch you, yet I hope at least that you will pardon a young composer who, his heart swollen and his imagination fired by your genius, has been unable to restrain this cry of admiration.

HECTOR BERLIOZ

Goethe, wrongly praised for his impassivity, which is a kind of inferiority..

VICTOR HUGO

Goethe, whose cunning would have made him the greatest genius of them all if genius could ever be a result of cunning; that clever deviser of settings, master of sharp practice in art, its means and its successes...

BARBEY D'AUREVILLY

Thus he was and remains the most indisputable genius of his century and perhaps of all the centuries of modern times on the other side of the Rhine, and even this side as well.

LAMARTINE

Goethe—there was a man! But *he* had everything—everything was on his side!

FLAUBERT

190

In his autobiography is Goethe, after all, ever doing anything but making a skilful defence of something worthless? At what point did he ever bring idea to reality? To use words in order to evade everything (women, the idea of love, that of Christianity, etc.) is what he excels in doing. Goethe does not, ultimately, differ except in degree from any criminal who similarly engages in fending off guilt by his ingenuity, holding it at bay by dint of myth-making.

KIERKEGAARD

Goethe is the last German for whom I feel respect.

NIETZSCHE

It is in the name of the Latin race to which I belong that I am taking to task the man who is, in literature, the best representative of the other race, in his cold, deductive, fragmentary, obscure genius, a product of assiduous labor and slow, mysterious advances, a genius without true inspiration, without ideals, without probity.

ALEXANDRE DUMAS FILS

... *anima naturaliter catholica* ...

PETER WUST

There is no more treacherous falsification of the figure of Goethe than that picture of serenity commonly made of him (at least in France). To hold impassively and smilingly aloof in a sort of happy superiority, in some region inaccessible to storm, is in no sense proper to him.

ANDRÉ GIDE

The whole of Goethe's genius is rooted in Being as in the very source of joy.

ROBERT D'HARCOURT

... that great solemn ass Goethe...

PAUL CLAUDEL

Under the romantic guise of Phoebus Apollo which has been attributed to him, the features of Apollo which he chiefly has are those of the exiled god, the lonely god, the god who fights the dragon but is too proud to boast of his battles and dangers, who fights alone, day by day re-enacting, alone, his ascent towards the light.

ROMAIN ROLLAND

... the European German, who turns towards the world a face which is indeed plainly German, but towards his own nation a face which is European...

THOMAS MANN

Goethe is like a great river, the Rhine itself, no longer a barrier but a link, an ever-living bridge between its two shores. He is the great reconciler between the Germanic world and the West.

ANDRÉ SUARÈS

That great man was, in truth, one of the luckiest throws that fate has ever allowed the human race to make upon the gaming-table of the world.

PAUL VALÉRY

'From one extreme to the other...' Goethe's comment on himself might equally well be made of the opinions held about him.

COVER PICTURE

A drawing made in November *1779*, during his visit to Switzerland, by the Zurich painter Johann Heinrich Lips, who collaborated with Lavater in his physiognomical work. Lavater's comment on this portrait:

"A head which proclaims its genius to all beholders! The brow is full of intelligence, the eye alight with fire. The nose is not large but fine, a mark of subtlety. The lip is capable of scorn and of searing power. The chin is somewhat full, the line of the head too low and straight."